AN HOUR TO THE STONE AGE

By
SHIRLEY HORNE

By
SHIRLEY HORNE

MOODY PRESS
CHICAGO

*To my three sons—Richard, Malcolm, and Stephen—
who counted separation from their parents as their
part in evangelizing the Dani people; as fellowship in
the sufferings of Christ, who left His Father that they,
the Danis, and all mankind might have eternal life.*

Many thanks to Ossie Emery and W. Turner for
their photographs used in this book.

© 1973 by
THE MOODY BIBLE INSTITUTE
OF CHICAGO

Library of Congress Catalog Card Number: 72-95020

ISBN: 0-8024-3690-0

Printed in the United States of America

Contents

ACKNOWLEDGMENTS

I am grateful to all who have helped to make the writing of this book possible: to Dr. Henry Brandt who first challenged me to write the story; to parents who have shared letters from their missionary children in West New Guinea; for tapes and letters from Charles Mellis and David Steiger of Missionary Aviation Fellowship, who played such a vital part in the initial air program; to missionary colleagues who took time to remember, patiently answer my questions, make tapes, and share records; to the Leiden University for furnishing me with facts of early history; for access to material from conferences of government and mission anthropologists; to Mrs. Miller and Mrs. McKelvie, Melbourne housewives, who typed the first draft of the manuscript; especially to Mrs. Murray Rule, M.A., who, when I was ready to give up, urged me on, and whose editing has helped to make this book what it is; to Celia Baker who kept giving me a "push" when I needed it most, and who, with my nieces Lorraine Rapp and Glenys Dunster, typed the finished manuscript; to my husband for answering endless questions, checking facts, dates, and directions, and to my family who shared precious holiday and furlough time with my writing.

To all these people I owe much and wish to acknowledge it.

Preface

PEOPLE WAITED. Others completed last minute business. Electric fans whirred, lazily stirring the hot heavy stillness. High heels click-clacked against concrete floors. Ice tinkled on glass; alcohol, cigarette smoke, and women's perfume mingled with the scent of tropical flowers twined around balustrades that kept wrought iron tables shaded and cool, contrasting with the hot, hard glare on the runway at Sentani airport in West New Guinea, where an aircraft from Australia unloaded passengers.

A warning voice broke through the ringing of telephones, rumbling of baggage-laden trolleys trundling through to the customs counters, and the thud of stamp against passport—"All passengers for the flight to Biak through to Hollandia, please proceed to board the aircraft."

A sudden buzz of a hundred voices said "good-bye" in Dutch, English, Indonesian, and Chinese.

The tower gave the all clear, and the giant aircraft lumbered into the sky on its way to Europe.

Following close behind it, a little yellow Cessna aircraft marked JZ-PTE, a call sign of the Missionary Aviation Fellowship, shot up the runway, rose sharply across Lake Sentani, and headed towards a blue smudge of mountains in the distant southwest. In one hour, after leaving all the sophistication of an international air terminal, the Cessna glided onto a mountain-locked airstrip. Soon it was surrounded by naked savages armed with Stone Age weapons.

Although separated by only an hour's flying time, neither the Stone Age group nor the gay, jostling crowd of the air terminal had any knowledge of the other. When one of the latter did hear of these people, she said, "I just didn't know that there were people like that still left in the world."

7

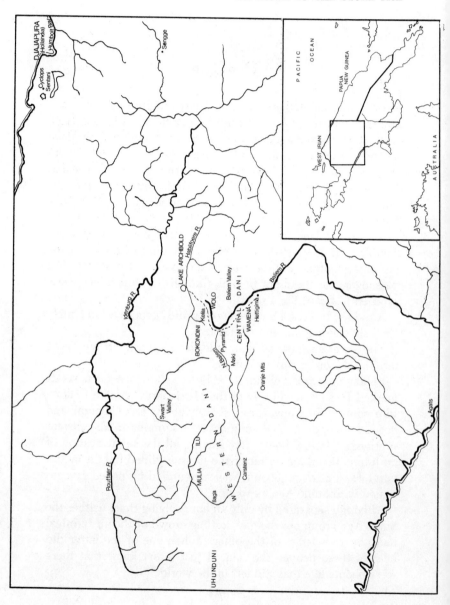

After living among the Stone Age Dani people of the West New Guinea Central Highlands for six years and seeing their abuse and scorn both for us and the gospel of Christ turn to love and acceptance, it was laid upon me to tell the story of that change.

In writing of the experiences of the Danis and the missionaries who lived among them, I have made no exaggerations, unless it be in understatement. Those were days of tension, suspense, and drama. As I saw in this mass movement—which, perhaps, has not been equaled in modern missionary experience—men like Jan and Unak who were turned from semihuman savages to men of dignity and gentleness through new life in Christ, I too, knew a greater breadth and depth of God's unfailing love and sovereign power. If while reading these pages, others should share this experience, my purpose in writing this book will have been fulfilled.

Let the [villages in the wilderness] lift up their voice . . . let the inhabitants of the rock sing, let them shout from the top of the mountains. Let them give glory unto the LORD, and declare His praise in the islands.

ISAIAH 42:11, 12

No man can enter into a strong man's house, and spoil his goods, except he will first bind the strong man; and then he will spoil his house.

MARK 3:27

For whosoever shall do the will of God, the same is my brother, and my sister.

MARK 3:35

1

The People Whom God Didn't Forget

TIME DRIFTED through the ages unmarked, uncounted. Round grass-thatched houses clung defiantly to ridges honed to saw-edged sharpness by rain and wind of centuries. Fences, flung across the steeps, kept pigs from extensive sweet potato gardens. Streams, white in their swiftness, descended to the brown twisting rivers of the lowlands.

A formation of Super Fortresses nosed out from behind a pile of mountains and eagled its way over the thatched villages, gardens, and rivers to its prey on the coast, one hour away.

The count of time had begun.

Dani men, their bodies smeared with pig grease and soot, knitted-string caps jammed on their matted hair, pig tusks forced through their noses, bundles of arrows and bows grasped in their hands, and stone axes slung over their shoulders, screwed their faces skyward against the sun. Naked children buried their dirty faces in their mothers' grass skirts.

"What is it? Why has it come?" hung unspoken among them. Fear in the women's eyes queried the men. The men flicked their bow strings and shook their heads. "We don't know. We haven't seen anything like it before."

Someone panicked and screamed. "Go inside! Go inside! Those are death things up there! We shall die!" Shrieking, they hurled themselves through doorways to huddle in the dark, sobbing and waiting for the "death things" to fall.

They *were* death things: bombers and fighter planes based in northern Australia and southern New Guinea. They flew

across the central highlands of West New Guinea, where the
great Dani tribe lived, to bomb the Japanese forces occupying
the north coast.

When the death things came almost daily across the sky, and
no death followed, popular opinion voted that they were the
"mother of steel." Didn't their great wings and bellies shine
like Attek's steel axe when it was twisted this way and that in
the sun? Wistfully, they hoped that the mother of steel would
send them more such axes.

In 1921 a Dutch expedition had passed through the Swart
Valley, climbed the fifteen thousand feet to the sometimes
snow-capped peak of Mount Wilhelmina and trekked back to
the coast through the North Baliem Valley.

The expedition, always moving on, had left little knowledge
with the western Danis as to who its members were and
from where they had come. Time had added the Dutchmen's
trek to the Dani legends. They became the offspring of Bok, a
mythical being who had come up out of the ground near the
Bejam Valley, before the western Danis came to the North
Baliem. Great footlike indentations pressed into the earth
were left as a testament of when he stood the mountains up and
poured out the rivers. Bok left the interior and went north-
wards to the coast. Crossing the ocean, he settled where the
heavens and earth met and the sun climbed a tree each morning before moving across the sky.

Bok's descendants had come; they had returned to the north
again; and all that remained was the steel axe, sharpened to a
splinter. And now the Danis had seen its mother.

They continued making sweet potato gardens, digging them
with sharpened sticks and fencing them with palings split with
stone axes. They slew their enemies with bamboo bows and
arrows or long palm spears. Then, smearing their bodies with
pig fat and soot, and donning headdresses of bird-of-paradise
plumes, flamboyant with a reckless extravagance of color, they
danced their victory *jewams*. At night they huddled in their
round houses away from the cold, the evil spirits, and prowling
marauders.

They repeated their folk stories and legends. Seated around their fires watching the women turn the potatoes baking on the glowing coals for their evening meal, children would demand of their fathers, "Tell us the story of how the Dani people came." Then the fathers would tell them how their people came up out of a hole in the ground.

First the ants bored a hole up from the bowels of the earth, and then one following another, they came up from the darkness into the sunlight and found it to be good.

After them came the snake making the hole larger and wriggling his long body through, into the new world of light. Every so often the snake slipped out of his dead skin to become a new and shining creature. Each time he shed his skin, he seemed to have the ability to put off death and to take on new life again. "He was immortal," the fathers told the children, "with him was the secret of eternal life. The snake intended to pass this secret on to man so that he too could shed his skin and go on living for ever." As the Dani people scraped away the earth, enlarging the hole, they pushed their way through and gathered around the snake who had waited to give them *nabelan kabelan*—"my outer skin, your outer skin"—eternal life.

Suddenly they heard a strange cry: *"Pirigoobit, pirigoobit."* They trembled at the strangeness of the sound, and fear entered into them. With the entrance of fear the process of death began upon their bodies, and the snake no longer had power to give them the immortal *nabelan kabelan.* Looking about them they saw a bird, and the bird, seeing that they were afraid and knowing that consequently they would experience death, began to gather and stack firewood in readiness to burn the bodies of the Danis when death claimed them.

"Then our first fathers cried with heartbreak and despair because they heard the cry of *"pirigoobit"* and became afraid, they lost the *nabelan kabelan,* and when they and all their descendants after them died, their spirits would go into the limestone caves in the mountains. And that is why," the fathers told their children, "that bird is called the *pirigoobit* and why we Dani people always burn our dead."

A vague story that someone from the 'west would come and bring them eternal life remained. Time had confused their memories, and long waiting had dulled their hope.

The fighters and bombers changed to freighters. The Danis noted the difference in aircraft but did not know that it resulted from the Allies recapturing the North Coast. Could they have seen the holocaust of modern war—the tangled wrecks of air, sea, and land transport—they would have claimed it the mother, father, and all the tribe of steel.

Gradually these flights discontinued and their hopes for steel axes were forgotten.

When the world heard about the highland dwellers, it called them "the people whom God forgot." But God had not forgotten them. He was preparing His men. Mission leaders were asking, "How can we get into the hinterland?" and "How can we maintain a supply line when we get in?" God was answering their prayerful questions.

In 1944 the Allies under General MacArthur forced the Japanese out of their temporary hold in the north coast of New Guinea. Bulldozers forged roads from Hollandia on Humboldt Bay, around the foot of the Cyclops Range to Sentani, where airstrips for Super Fortresses were built.

MacArthur set up his headquarters at Ifar on the Cyclops Mountains, a thousand feet above the humidity of the plains. Military hospitals were established at Ifar, Kota Nica, and Kota Baru. The American Air Force spread its camp at the base of Mt. Cyclops. Instead of the handful from the previous peacetime occupation—government officers, missionaries, and traders—the area now swarmed with American troops.

American Air Force personnel flying back and forth across the interior took a lively interest in the valley which Richard Archbold had found in 1938. They pored excitedly over new copies of the National Geographic magazine which carried the account of the expedition. In the turmoil and anxiety of war into which the world had been plunged, Baliem Valley was forgotten by the public. Only scientists, anthropologists, and

DANI MAN. One of "God's forgotten people" displays elaborately coiled hairdo.

missionaries tucked it away in their memories as a field to be worked when the war was over.

Now the American Air Force had "found" it for themselves. In the mess halls and recreation rooms, talk of rugged mountain splendor, fertile valleys, and thousands of grass huts housing "God's forgotten people" relieved operation tensions.

Curiosity of the ground personnel had been so excited by these reports that the Army administration arranged flights inland for them on leave days. Anyone who had the opportunity, GIs or WACs, were keen to go on these trips.

Dina Reimeyer, Dutch by birth, but a Canadian by naturalization, had joined up with the Netherlands Army in Montreal. In early 1945 she was posted to a hospital at Kota Nica in West New Guinea.

On May 13 she was invited to go on one of these Sunday trips inland. She was eager to see this place and to get away from the heat and monotony of the camp, but a GI, her current date, pressed her to spend her Sunday with him instead. To please him, she reluctantly relinquished her place in the plane.

The big C-47 that had taken off that day with twenty-four light-hearted people on board never returned. It crashed in the pass of the Oranje Mountains.

Danis, hopeful of what they might discover, climbed to where the "mother of steel" had fallen. Fear, bred of superstition, gripped them. It was a death thing indeed. It had killed itself spewing out death. Twenty-one bodies lay thrown about.

In the midst they found three persons alive and badly hurt. Natural sympathy overcame their fear. They lit a fire to warm the injured, built a shelter to protect them, and came often with food. Their friendly concern encouraged and comforted the survivors.

Search planes located the crash. Food and clothing were dropped. Medical corps men parachuted to treat the three injured ones. How to get them out posed quite a problem to the American Air Force. As a standard airplane could not land in the vicinity, they decided to launch a glider with the use of a towplane. Men and equipment were parachuted to the site chosen for the operation. The two men and the woman, with her wounded, gangrenous legs, were taken over the mountain trail to where Filipino paratroopers had built a glider strip.

The plane, with glider in tow, roared over the mountains, completing the rescue which had drawn heavily on the ingenuity and purse of the American Air Force.

During the seventeen days in the Oranje Mountains—now Soekarno Mountains—the trio had known the grandeur and majesty of the country, the everlasting spring climate, and the friendliness of a primitive people. Experience was to prove these people most unfriendly under different circumstances.

War correspondents soon published stories of a "Shangri-la" in the central highland of West New Guinea, stirring the imaginations of adventurous readers throughout the world. Young men and women with missionary vision became concerned over these people locked in the mountains.

Dina Reimeyer was thankful to God for keeping her from that disastrous trip. Although not then a committed Christian, the needs of these people challenged her. Deep in her heart was a yearning to return when the war was over.

And she did come back—this time with her husband, David Cole. As missionaries with the Unevangelized Fields Mission, they started the work on the Iluwagi River, on the slopes of the Central Divide which separated them from the main Baliem, or "Shangri-la," Valley.

Robert J. Story, then general secretary of the Unevangelized Fields Mission (UFM) for Australia and New Zealand, read the stories and preserved them along with the accounts of Richard Archbold's expedition into the Valley. His determination to enter the country was even more fired by this report.

2

Finding a Foothold

SHAPED LIKE a giant prehistoric bird with its claws resting at the tip of Australia's northern Cape York, its head nestling in the Spice Islands, and its tail flipping the western shores of the Solomons, New Guinea stretches below the equator.

Through the years she has tenaciously guarded her secrets with weapons of disease, loneliness, and privation, repelling the curious explorer, greedy profiteer, sacrificing settler, and zealous missionary.

"New Guinea is a land of contrasts" is a cliché which nevertheless cannot be denied. Picture poster beaches, under softly swaying palms, are lapped by blue waters in the east and north. In the south and west, crocodile-infested mangrove swamps, heavy with the fetor of rot and stagnation, end in thick black mud at the water's edge.

These same steaming, fetid swamps spread through dreary miles of savanna country right to the center of the island. Here, they suddenly give place to thousands of feet of rugged mountain grandeur, gentle slopes, and deep valleys gouged out by severe erosion. Like a backbone dividing the country, this central chain of mountains runs almost the entire length of New Guinea.

On the coast, sophisticated tropical towns have grown up where many Papuans, the natives of New Guinea, in starched shirts and bright dresses have entered the business and educational world.

In outstations, under primitive conditions, government officers struggle to bring savage tribes under control. Tucked

18

away in little pockets, the untouched tribes still wait for the outside world to open to them.

The Papuans are animists worshipping the spirits of their ancestors, who they believe have power to strengthen, guard, and provide for them. They are bound by fetters of fear, spirit worship, and fate.

Before World War II only the geographical minded knew that New Guinea was divided into three sections. By treaty in 1895 a line was drawn across the center of the island dividing the east from the west. West of this boundary was the area known as Netherlands New Guinea, belonging to the Dutch until May 1, 1963, when the red and white flag of Indonesia was hoisted in towns and lonely outposts.

The eastern half of New Guinea is divided into two parts. The northern section, originally occupied by Germany, is now the Trust Territory of New Guinea under a United Nations mandate to Australia. The southern division, Papua, is a territory of Australia. Both are administered from Port Moresby and are preparing for self-government and independence.

At the border of West New Guinea is the great Fly River which flows through the miasmal swamp and jungle center of southwest Papua to empty daily thousands of tons of water into the Gulf of Papua. Headhunters living along its course hung the smoked heads of victims and relatives in their long-houses; lived on what sago, fish, and game the country yielded; and paddled their dugout canoes through the labyrinth of waterways. In 1931 the UFM began work in New Guinea and sent their first missionary to these Fly River people. The work spread. The mission boat *Maino II* plied up and down the river with personnel and supplies. As the boat rounded the bend at the border, those aboard would ask, "What about those spreading away across from the western banks? When shall they hear the gospel?"

In the southeastern foothills of the Star Mountains, missionaries asked the same questions concerning those on the other side of the ranges faintly outlined in the distance. Observation of custom and language indicated that the people on both

sides of the range had a common origin. At their conferences
the missionaries discussed, as a future project, the evangeliza-
tion of these people.

Meanwhile, seven years of missionary service in Brazilian
forests had sapped Robert Story's health. He returned home to
become general secretary of the Australian and New Zealand
branch of the Unevangelized Fields Mission. Although his
active service on the field had ceased, his concern for the un-
converted had by no means waned. He was right with the
missionaries on the field in finding new areas and breaking a
way into them.

Maps of New Guinea hung on his office wall. His eyes continually sought the unknown, mysterious central highland of
West New Guinea. Al Lewis, aircraft pilot for Christian and
Missionary Alliance, and Robert Story enjoyed a long friendship based on their common desire to see the south coast of
West New Guinea and adjacent regions opened to the gospel
of Christ. Together they sought out all the available informa-
tion on the west.

In June, 1949, Robert Story received a warm invitation from
the United Dutch Missions to enter the unevangelized areas
of Dutch New Guinea. In the list of areas opened, the Baliem
and Swart Valleys were named.

The American section of UFM began showing interest in
New Guinea and offered to send Americans after the Australians opened up the field.

Fred Dawson, a heavily built western Australian and graduate of Perth Bible Institute, offered to go in to get the work
started. He had only three years' field experience. He kissed
good-bye his bride of three months and set out in September,
1950, on an extremely difficult mission, for which, humanly
speaking, he was unprepared.

At Port Moresby, on the southeast coast, he met Robert
Story and they flew together to Wewak on the northern coast.
These were pioneering days—days of making do, days when
there were few alternate airstrips and no fuel depots at most
of them, days when fuel for the return trip was part of the

essential loading. Jammed in among baggage and the drums filled with aviation gas, the two men were almost overcome with the fumes which escaped the loosely fitting caps. The pilot, nonchalantly reading a yellow paperback, looked up every fifteen to twenty minutes to check his position. Following the jungle coastline they flew west over wartime airfields pitted by bombs and strewn with mangled aircraft. Out over Hollandia Harbor, they looked out on the vivid blue beauty of the bay scarred by half-sunken boats, tilted grotesquely in death. Barges rusted on the golden sands. They landed at Sentani's American-built airstrip surrounded by debris of war—the junk and wreckage of aircraft abandoned to the tropical elements.

From Joka, Story and Dawson surveyed the north coastal regions not already worked by the Dutch Reformed Church. The untouched population was scattered and sparse.

An audience with the governor of Netherlands New Guinea did not encourage hope of immediate opening in the heavily populated but uncontrolled interior. The situation appeared impossible. They were too soon. There was nowhere to start work and no way of getting into the interior.

Beyond the quiet waters of the lake, with a village rising on stilts from its shores, rose the blue line of distant mountains. Behind those mountains, in valley after valley, thousands of Papuans waited for eternal life. The two men looked for a way to reach them.

"Fred," said Bob Story, "the Lord has not burdened our hearts for this country in vain. He has not led us out to shut the door in our faces." They knew that the Lord does not stand security for failure; neither was He telling them to batter down the closed door, but to "wait on the Lord and He will give you the desires of your heart." By faith they believed that the interior of New Guinea would open to them.

The aircraft which took Robert Story out brought Margaret Dawson in. This compensated Dawson for the loss of his colleague. Margaret was in every sense a helpmeet. She entertained church and government officials in equatorial heat, with

its overpowering lethargy, without household help and essential amenities. She shared her husband's problems with discernment and encouragement.

Fred and Margaret Dawson spent the first two months at
Genjem, an outpost of Joka. They chafed to get out, find a
site, and start their own work. But the "Wet" (monsoon sea-
son) had started and imprisoned them at Genjem. They applied
themselves to learning Malay. Dawson, foraging around in
rubbish dumps where the wrecks of war had been deposited,
unearthed a jeep. He made frequent trips to the dumps to find
the parts necessary to put it into running order. When the jeep
was finished, almost to the day, the dumps closed. With the
jeep the Dawsons had gained a certain independence and now
had transport to the business center twenty miles away.

They planned to find areas of work south of Hollandia which
they would use as stepping stones into the interior. After a trek
of ten days' hard walking south through dense rain forest, they
came out at Sengge, a hundred miles from Genjem. Here they
found a closely settled population and, after measuring and
pegging out an airstrip, spent a week cutting the grass and
starting on the construction of a house. This, they hoped, would
become the base for their entry into the interior.

Reinforcements were soon to arrive, however, so the Dawsons had to leave their newly laid foundations and hurry back
to the coast to meet three new missionaries—Russell Bond and
his fiancée Lil Bryan from New Zealand, and Val Jones from
South Australia. They were as excited as children as they
drove from Genjem, turned the jeep into the Sentani airstrip,
and waited for the hum of the airplane bringing their own
people to them. After Customs was finished, they loaded the
jeep and trailer with their luggage and also stores which had
been brought from Australia. Food was expensive and scarce.
One ship a month and one plane a week were the only supply
services in operation; and their cargoes were barely sufficient
to maintain the population, which included hundreds of Eura-
sian refugees from Indonesia. Food was heavily rationed.
Those who could purchase bread were not permitted a flour

ration. Powdered milk was only obtainable by a special permit through the hospital. Food supplies came to the missionaries through uncertain, often dangerous routes. Mail arrived infrequently.

With the arrival of three new missionaries, a new house had somehow to be obtained, but the only one available was a native-style house at Joka on Sentani Lake. As the previous occupant, a Papuan teacher, moved his boxes out, the missionaries moved theirs in. The accumulation of dirt, the hordes of cockroaches, and swarms of flies appalled them. Buckets of hot soapy water and hard scrubbing made some improvement, but it was impossible to remove from the thatched walls all the filth of years. Here, perhaps, were the beginning of continued illnesses from amoebic dysentery.

While Nurse Lillian Bryan gained experience in tropical medicine at the general hospital, Jones and Bond made the long trek back down to Sengge to complete the airstrip started by Dawson. It was clear that a supply line over the difficult and dangerous trail could not be maintained, and Dawson looked for a house near the Sentani airfield. An old, large hostel owned by an airline company was loaned them. Rat-infested and dilapidated, it contained wonderful amounts of storage space.

Although the hostel provided urgently needed temporary accommodation, a permanent headquarters near the airfield was still needed. Early one morning, after devotions outdoors in a quiet spot down the hill, Dawson arose to return home. He was arrested by the great amount of rusting iron and rotting timber lying about on the ground. "Surely this is an old army site," he mused. He scuffed at the loose sand with the toe of his shoe; then, thoroughly interested, he scatched around until he was certain that underneath the debris and weeds lay a huge slab of concrete. A thought streaked through his mind. Returning after breakfast with a shovel, he uncovered twenty by fifty yards of cement. Awed, he stood and claimed it in faith as the future UFM headquarters.

Cooperation by the Papuan owners and approval by the

Dutch government made it the UFM's by permanent lease. Eventually an attractive and suitable base house was erected.

In the meantime, the airstrip at Sengge had not been built without incident. Jones, alone on the job while Bond had trekked to Sentani for supplies, went down with blackwater fever and almost died. Aircraft from the Australia territory, chartered to drop supplies, often dropped from too high, and the bulk of the supplies were either lost or irreparably damaged. Russell Bond and Lillian Bryan were married at Sentani at the close of 1952, and despite the unfinished strip, Russell brought his bride to a little thatched log cabin in the jungle two days from Sengge. An American family, the Veldhuises, joined Val Jones at Sengge, and further reinforcements came up from Australia and New Zealand.

Once the strip was completed towards the end of 1953, supplies started coming in by plane, and the situation improved. Medical clinics were begun, schools were opened, Bible study classes and church services were held; and as a result, Sengge men and women received Christ and were baptized into His church.

The missionaries began to realize that the establishment of the church at Sengge was a major stepping-stone to the highlands. From these people who were once afraid to move outside their own villages came dedicated men to go with the missionaries into the unknown interior. Without their help the entry could not have been done.

3

Pathfinder Opens the Way

In 1952, while the Sengge airstrip was under construction, Grady Parrott, director of the North American MAF (Missionary Aviation Fellowship), visited Australian New Guinea. He wanted to help the Australian MAF reestablish their flying program following the crash of the first plane and the death of its pilot. The Missionary Aviation Fellowship, begun by war pilots after the war to help missionaries in isolated areas, started its program in Mexico and the jungles of Ecuador. The MAF boys had seen the *National Geographic* articles on Archbold's discoveries and the exciting press coverages of the glider rescue of the three American Air Force personnel from "Shangri-la." As far back as 1947, Nate Saint, the MAF pilot murdered by the Auca Indians, had written from Wheaton College to his brother Sam about the New Guinea project.

In following years, missionary men had asked the MAF for assistance in reaching the remote valley people of the West New Guinea central highlands. Invited to visit Dawson at Sentani, Grady Parrott accepted.

The Christian and Missionary Alliance abandoned their original idea of moving into the Baliem overland from the Wissel Lakes. They established a base at Sentani from which to operate; at the same time, The Evangelical Alliance Mission (TEAM) was also looking for a way into the Baliem.

So it was that Dawson and Bond from UFM, Jerry Rose from C&MA, and Walter Erikson from TEAM held long conferences with the North American MAF director. But without knowing what lay beyond the mountains, definite plans could not be made. Thus, with government permission, they chartered a small Norseman to take them on a survey of the interior. A Dutch air official accompanied them.

As the Norseman roared its engines, quivered, gathered itself together and rose into the air, the spirits of the men soared with it, over Lake Sentani and the flat sago swamps breathing heavy moisture into low hung clouds, and out toward the mountains, mysterious against the skyline. Soon they would cross their bulwarks and discover their tenaciously held secrets. Now they would see some of the impossibilities—could they meet the challenge?

For three hours they flew; glimpsed the flooded Idenberg writhing towards the sea; followed the Hablifoerie into Lake Archbold; viewed the lake where Archbold's amphibian had already made a successful landing; crossed the Dinggun Ridge and the Boko River. Rugged, terrible mountains massed in majestic grandeur, enduring the centuries, stood silent, indifferent to the puny airplane. Tree tops on wooded slopes lay below like heads of coral growing from exposed reefs. Bold, sharp-edged ridges rose like barricades of upturned swords forbidding an entry.

Round mushroomlike houses surrounded by extensive cultivation clung to slopes and crowded the valley floors. Hundreds and hundreds of them in valley after valley. They indicated people, a teeming population made up of individuals—each man and woman with a personal need. It was for them that the eyes from the airplane windows were searching.

The Danis looked up and saw, after all the years of an empty sky, another "death thing." How could they know that this aircraft carried the messengers of life?

The Norseman negotiated the rugged pass and flew straight down the main Baliem Valley to pyramid-shaped rocks rising steeply out of the flat valley. All along the way were houses, gardens, and people—150,000 Stone Age people waiting for eternal life!

The missionaries scanned the ground for likely airstrip sites. The Dutchman made a sweeping statement. "It's impossible—absolutely impossible to build an airstrip in the interior." The missionaries felt a reluctant inclination to agree with him. Vast sheets of water covered the Baliem Valley. One grassy strip south of the pyramid rocks held the only possibility—but it seemed to be in a no-man's-land. It could be used only as a base, for no population closed in against it.

The missionaries did not know that the Baliem was in abnormally high flood, not since repeated. Since that initial survey, more than thirty interior airstrips have been built and operated upon by MAF in some amazing places: cut into sides of a mountain, perched high on a windswept plateau, or flanked by the sheer drop of a canyon.

The Norseman nosed up towards the Swart Valley. The pilot glanced uneasily at the dark rain-filled clouds massing on the ridges. Fuel was running low. They carried no radio. Reluctantly they turned and headed towards the pass and Sentani.

Their minds, hearts, and Kodachrome rolls were filled with the enormity of what they had seen. Each heart cried out, "When can we go?" Each will resolved to exert a more determined effort. Each man knew the puniness of his own strength against the physical and spiritual bulwarks opposing him.

Each man's faith was in the power of the Christ who said, "As the Father has sent me, so send I you."

When Grady Parrott left Sentani, each missionary pressed him with the same question, "When will you be able to get an air program operating?"

Grady replied, "I can't promise anything except that we'll work on it and strain our utmost to get into this thing with you."

Within a year of the fatal plane accident, the MAF service in the Australia Territory was reinstated. Lanky Charles Mellis settled at Madang with his wife Clare in June, 1963. Communication between the eastern and western sections of New Guinea was still slow and roundabout. No commercial airline flew across the border. In October, however, Mellis managed to get on a charter flight to Hollandia and threw himself into a round of interviews with Dutch officials. A final audience with the governor was encouraging.

Before Mellis left Hollandia, reports were coming in that Erikson and Tritt of TEAM, who had left Manokwari on trek in mid-September, had been murdered. A police patrol, sent out by the Dutch government, returned to verify the reports. They had found the bodies of the two men near the Ainim River. While they had slept, their carriers, consumed with greed, slashed at them with machetes. With their bare hands the men had tried to ward off the attackers but had been overpowered. Tritt fell and died at the place of attack. Erikson, horribly mutilated, had crawled to a cave in the mountain where, suffering excruciating pain, he died alone. With a heightened realization of the urgent need for air support for the missionaries, Mellis soberly returned to Madang.

When word was received in the United States of the martyrdom of Erikson and Tritt, the students of the Columbia Bible College were deeply stirred. Voluntarily and sacrificially they raised funds to provide for MAF an aircraft which would eliminate some of the arduous and dangerous trekking. As it was unknown what type of aircraft would be most suitable or what operations it would be involved in, a Piper-Pacer was purchased and was fitted for both wheels and pontoons before being sent to Sentani. It was named the *Pathfinder*. Its arrival was a great occasion and it was greeted like a celebrity by the missionaries who felt that at last they were assured of security in their line of supplies and communications.

Although at that time only UFM and TEAM were to use the plane, (C&MA having initiated its own air program), MAF headquarters had agreed with Charles Mellis that an aircraft should be based and registered in West New Guinea even though it would have to be subsidized. The first pilot was David Steiger. David and his vivacious wife Janet moved into Sentani in March, 1955, residing first in the rat-infested one-time hostel, but later setting up home in a prefabricated aluminum house bolted onto one of the vacant concrete slabs unearthed on the old Air Force campsite by the UFM men. With UFM, C&MA, and MAF establishing base houses here, this slope up to Cyclops Mountains became known as Mission Hill.

Up to this time, it was the ruling of the Dutch New Guinea government that missions could not precede the government into areas where there were no established government posts. The Roman Catholic missions made representation to the large Roman Catholic political party in Holland. This resulted in a bill, put before parliament by this party, being passed giving unrestricted movement to all mission societies.

The *Pathfinder*, fitted with floats, made a highway into the interior. The little Pacer, bobbing like a beetle on the smooth Sentani Lake, could be mistaken for a rich man's pleasure craft. To the long thwarted missionaries it had the wings of an angel.

Some said, "It's too small. Too unsafe. That type of country requires of a plane at least two engines." But the little *Pathfinder* probed the unknown, battled great storm heads, forced a way through murky mists, soared into the limitless blue—free and joyous, bringing a message of hope.

One man, one engine, one God. As long as God was in control, the man was satisfied.

4

First Contact–and a Stabbed Pig

THE BALIEM RIVER had dropped to an unsafe landing level. Pilot and party to survey the interior were in regular radio contact with the missionaries at Hettigima, the C&MA base camp in the Baliem. The survey party's departure date for the inland had been set for Saturday, January 22, 1955, but on the preceding Friday morning the water was still two feet below minimum safe level.

Four o'clock that afternoon, a voice came in jubilantly from Hettigima, "The river has risen two feet. There's heavy rain on the mountains and the water's still rising. Guess if the weather's good we'll be seeing you tomorrow."

Anticipation mounted. Evening prayers in each family circle were for fine weather and touched with the tenderness of farewell before the long and unknown separation.

All December and January, the three men chosen for the survey patrol into the inland–Hans Veldhuis, Fred Dawson, and Russell Bond–had prepared. They had spent many nights studying conditions and poring over maps which would strengthen the strategy of their penetration into the interior. What they had heard and read didn't whet their appetites. Bond's trek around behind Sengge had taken him into uncontrolled territory, but the other two men had not been beyond the limits of government influence. None had previously encountered people like the unrestrained Danis.

The Dutch government made available reports and maps of the Archbold expedition.

They tested the radio, made up packs for themselves and the carriers for the first two weeks; each man would carry sixty pounds. They took photographs of their families and packed three months' supply of food ready for air drops.

Fourteen men and a married couple with two children volunteered to accompany the three missionaries into the highlands. They were all Sengge people not long converted from heathenism. The love of God, the joy of their new faith, the desire to share it—some spirit of adventure—all stirred within them. The family—church elder Daniel, his wife and their six-year-old Mes and year-old Bok—went to give the patrol an air of friendliness; to give the Danis cause to realize that they were not marauders, but settlers.

The Christian and Missionary Alliance had inaugurated their own aviation program with a Sealander twin-engined amphibian aircraft. In April 1954 C&MA made their initial flight into the Shangri-la or Grand Valley, as it was now more commonly called, and landed on the Baliem River. In the spearhead party had been the Papuan missionary, Elisa, a man from the Kapauku tribe of the Wissel Lakes, and Myron Bromley, a linguist, whose job was to break the language barrier between the missionaries and the little-known Danis whom they hoped to win for Christ.

Meanwhile the UFMers had stood behind that first advance by prayer, while experiencing a very human impatience to move into the interior themselves. When it had been certain that the MAF *Pathfinder* was on its way to West New Guinea, they had planned their inland advance around available opportunities, depending on MAF to be ready to maintain their supply line by the time they were established in the highlands.

Their long, slow struggle with the Sengge airstrip and their failure to discover suitable strip sites during the air survey discouraged them from anything but a float operation, to be based on Lake Archbold. The C&MA Sealander pilot was not prepared to land on the lake as the Archbold Expedition had done seventeen years earlier in a higher powered aircraft. Swaths of trees at each end of the lake cut the take-off distance to below marginal length. He would fly them to the long straight stretch of the Baliem river at the lower end of the valley where the

C&MA had made their first landing and established the Hettigima mission camp. From here the UFMers would walk to Lake Archbold, establish their base, and penetrate into the valleys north, east, and southwest.

On that Saturday morning in January as the Sealander revved up its engines, Veldhuis looked at his watch—7:50 A.M. The men raised their hands in salute to their families. Their hearts were full. The warmth of embrace and their children's soft kisses still lingered with them. Prayers too deep to voice— that they would be a family again—reached up to God. Barely conscious that the plane was in the air, they held their loved ones within their gaze until they were a blur in the distance.

They flew southwest. A flat white sea of morning clouds stretched below them. It cleared, giving place to jungle cut by writhing waterways collected into one by the Idenberg on its winding westward course. Massive bulwalks of the divide rose against them. They slipped through the pass and headed towards Archbold Lake. From here the pilot flew along the route which the party would take back to the lake. They strained to pick up landmarks.

At nine-thirty the Sealander splashed down on the river, sweeping away a white flying spray of water. The fellows scrambled out and stamped their feet on inland soil.

The Sealander taxied to take-off position to bring more men and equipment from the coast. The amphibian screamed down the river. A sudden tearing and jarring thrust the crew forward as the craft lashed against the control. She ploughed into the water, pitching and slewing against sudden resistance. Water poured through the floorboards.

They beached the Sealander on the river bank and pulled out the flooring. A gaping hole had been ripped in the hull by a sandbank in midstream. They baled out the boat and pushed sheets of aluminum down hard against the tear. With the engineer forcing a bag against the repair, the pilot taxied up the river and took off.

By Wednesday noon all the UFM party were in the Baliem. They spent a couple of days under canvas orientating them-

TRIBAL FEAST. Dani tribesmen prepare pigs for ceremonial feasting.

selves to the climate and people, as well as learning a few basic Dani words from Bromley, the C&MA linguist stationed at Hettigima. The sudden change to high altitude cold from tropical heat had resulted in gastric upsets for some.

A dignified Dani chief, resplendent in the white and yellow cockatoo feathers of his office, smeared with pig fat and smelling like a smoked ham, responded to the coming of so many guests with true Papuan hospitality. He killed his fatted pig and entertained the party with a feast.

Nods and smiles, the universal language, assured both groups that all was well, despite the warlike appearance of their Dani hosts, who had come in full military dress; feather, pig-tusk nose decoration and soot-blackened faces with the resulting sinister expressions. Each man wore a pubic gourd of varying length and carried an assortment of arms: 12-foot spears, bows and arrows, stone axes, and bone daggers. The wary tension, which never left the Danis, kept the party from being deceived by their ingratiating smiles.

Nevertheless, with a sense of well-being, the men were astir early in the morning of Friday 28. Tents were taken down and folded, equipment gathered and secured to the carrying frames. One Sengge man took the seventy-pound tent. By 6:45 A.M. the men were ready to move. Bromley, who wished to go up the valley to do a language check, availed himself of the party's company. They in turn welcomed his knowledge of the language and the people. Elisa, the Kapauku missionary, accompanied Bromley.

The men gathered, committed themselves to God, and headed up the valley towards the northwest. The Danis, hooting and shouting, ran beside the men. Tugging at their loads they begged to carry the packs. When successful in grabbing something, they would dash triumphantly ahead. To let them help made it impossible to keep track of the gear. They split the ranks of the carriers and harried and embarrassed the lone woman whom they wanted to buy for cowrie shell and pig.

They passed over foothills, undulating grass country, with an occasional steep spur jutting out from the main range. They had chosen the mountain trail rather than the easier valley floor to avoid the masses of people who populated the Grand Valley. On either side stretched crops of potatoes, trenched, terraced, and fenced with split palings from four to five feet high to keep pigs from the sweet roots. In single file they followed the pad track through the gardens. Clambering over the fences with the heavy packs on their backs slowed them down and gave the Danis added opportunity to make off with their loads.

After leaving the first group of Danis, who were more nuisance than trouble, they passed through a stretch of empty ground into another group. These, though noticeably more obnoxious and daring, caused no real difficulty.

Reaching the Wamena River they crossed over on two stout lengths of lawyer cane laced with poles, swinging crazily between trees on either side of the stream. At two o'clock they made camp on the northern bank.

Wide-eyed Danis milled about, fascinated by the erection of the tent and camp preparations. They handled everything, leaving greasy black finger marks and a strong odor of smoked pig fat. The people pressed sweet potatoes onto the campers in return for cowrie shell. Suppurating ulcers and festering sores were cause for the hypodermic syringe and penicillin. Unprotesting, Danis presented their buttocks to the jab of the needle and its promised healing.

In the late afternoon the stench of burning hair and scorching flesh fouled the mountain air. The Danis had dragged two squealing pigs into camp in exchange for fifteen cowrie shells and a hatchet. The creamy, polished cowrie shell is a medium of exchange among the New Guineans, who use it in their ceremonies.

The men conferred together. "How are we going to kill them? If we shoot them, we might arouse more than we bargained for."

Dawson held up his knife and went through the pantomime of stabbing a pig. The people nodded and smiled in understanding. Thinking he had their approval, he stuck the animal. As its blood spurted, the Danis sprang to their feet, pranced, yelled, and pulled at their bow strings. Their agitated feathers swayed wildly; their eyes gleamed. Raised voices proclaimed their intense disapproval.

The men looked at each other in dismay. They had obviously cut across a sacred rite. They tried to pacify the hysterical group. They talked—and the Danis yelled. Wisely or not, they handed out more cowrie shells and the tension eased. But what they feared had been proved; Danis once aroused do not quieten easily. They became even more demanding.

"All right, you fellows, kill the second pig your way," the missionaries said.

A Dani rushed forward and grabbed the squealing pig by the forelegs, while another took hold of the hind legs. A third Dani, standing a foot away, fitted an arrow to his bow, let fly, and pierced the pig in the heart. Its carcass was then thrown on the fire to singe off the hair. They watched the body swell

and stiffen as the air reeked. Then they gutted the animal,
cut the flesh into chunks, and threw them onto the coals.

The pigs had been bought for the carriers' evening meal. As
the Sengge men turned the pork, watching the red juices flow,
the savory essence of cooking meat teased their appetites
sharpened by the long climb. The Danis too were hungry, and
their manners did not prevent them from helping themselves
to the cooking meat, which they themselves had sold on the
hoof. Although the carriers protested against the disappearnce
of their meal, attempts to prevent it were futile in the confusion of a camp full of excited Danis.

The party camped on the edge of a no-man's-land, a stretch
of empty country between two warring parties, and left early
the next morning before the crowd was about. Passing through
the vacant land towards the Ibele Valley, another horde of
Danis came out to meet them. Shouting, wildly brandishing
weapons, and waving their arms, they pressed in closely on
either side of the carrier line. Pulling their clothing, plucking
at their skin and peering into their faces, they worried the
trekkers almost to exhaustion. As they climbed with their packs
between two low ridges, a Dani grabbed a bush knife from a
Sengge man and dashed off. Immediately the crowd scattered
up the sides of the ridges. Lined along the top, standing against
the skyline, they hurled stones and abuse at the line of men
caught in the narrow path below them.

Outwardly ignoring them, but fearful of what might result,
the party moved through the defile and struck a midday bivouac by a small creek. Knowing that their preservation lay in
their mastery of every situation with the Danis, they deemed
it strategic to recover the stolen knife. Dani volunteers took
them to several huts, deceptively claiming each to be the home
of the culprit, before they finally caught up with the thief.
After much palaver, threats, and a little show of force, the
culprit returned the knife.

Too late in the afternoon to move on, they pitched their
camp where they had bivouacked. The next day being Sunday,
they stayed in camp. Danis boldly pushed in upon them, chal-

lenging their authority to demand the return of the knife. They pulled down parts of the campers' makeshift fence, crawled through the grass to their tents, and tried to squirm under the canvas in an attempt to steal. They threatened the carriers and had one down, menacing him with a spear at his throat. A sudden sharp rainstorm abruptly ended the melee and sent the marauders scampering to their villages.

The men voiced their relief and gratitude to God, but slept uneasily. They decided not to pitch a rest camp again in a heavily populated area. Early at four o'clock they broke camp, ate their breakfast, and were prepared to leave as soon as dawn lit their path.

Dawn led them out into hilly country sloping steeply towards the Ibele on the south side. With the sun burning on their laden backs, they took frequent rests under the scattered clumps of trees left by the Dani farmers when they had cleared for the extensive cultivations spreading on all sides. Climbing beans twisted around stakes driven into the black soil in measured rows made Russell Bond think with a nostalgic pang of the Chinese market gardens back in Auckland.

The trekkers, relaxed from the tensions of the jostling crowds, enjoyed the friendly curiosity of the women who came out of their gardens to watch them pass and to offer gifts of sugarcane and cucumbers. Sunshine bathed the rolling grasslands in rich color. A profusion of wild flowers—ground orchids, flame colored rhododendrons, and pretty, but tasteless wild raspberries—swift brooks shadowed by vinedraped trees—the green basin of the Baliem Valley skylined by rugged mountains topped with fleecy clouds against vivid blue—all this exhilarated the trekkers, tempting them to forget their isolation.

The hills drummed with the reverberating calls of the Danis as the party descended steeply into the great population of the Ibele Valley which joins the Baliem at the northern end. They knew that they had been sighted and that soon Dani company would be pressing in upon them.

At noon they dropped their packs onto a sandy bank of the river, flexed their muscles, and flopped onto the sun-warmed rocks. Fierce, sullen warriors armed with long spears, some standing, some squatting on their haunches, warily watched every movement of the strangers. Tired as they were, the men could not relax under their calculating gaze.

"We'll have to push on if we are to make camp before the rains come," said Veldhuis, struggling into his pack.

They prepared to go down a spur jutting out on the northern side of the Ibele into the Grand Valley and turning up into the main valley itself. The people, determined to lead them out into the Ibele Valley, argued with them and barred the way with spears. Finally, they yielded, lowered their spears, and let the party pass through the scrub dividing the gardens from the uninhabited area.

Dawson and the carriers made camp on a grassy hillock near a little stream, while Veldhuis and Bond accompanied Bromley back to a village to work on the language check which he was making as he traveled. Seeing their approach, Dani guards raised an alarm. Villagers took up the cry and with arms at the ready, swooped down the hill towards the three men. Some yards off they massed together. A few of the older men put up their arms and edged cautiously forward to inquire the intruders' business. A band of eager teenage would-be warriors, greased and feathered, and with oiled hair twisted into long curls flopping around their faces, dashed across the creek, brandishing their spears. With sweating bodies quivering, they crowded in upon the white men. Russell Bond, trying hard not to notice the spear point held ready for action at the base of his neck by an agitated youth, concentrated on the old men. Bromley used all the language he knew to explain why they had come back.

"We've not come to fight, steal, or molest your women. We want to learn your language so that we can talk with you and be your friends."

They seemed to get the idea, but it was five minutes before the lad with the spear relaxed enough to put it down.

After getting words and persuading them to bring food to the camp, the men returned to find that Dawson had established camp and had put out the radio antenna on the northern side between the camp and a grassy knoll.

A cluster of spears then faces daubed with white bands, showed above the scrub a little way off. The campers froze, fear in their throats, questioning their intent. The Danis stopped, warily watching the white men, then realizing that they were seen, trotted up to the camp. They stopped at the radio antenna, looked at it, and talked about it. Confused, they walked up and down the wire, searching for a way through. The men relaxed, the Danis were obviously friendly but had prepared for the worst. They had thought that the wire was some magic put out to protect the camp and to effect harm upon themselves.

Five days later Myron Bromley and Elisa turned back to Hettigima. The two lone travelers were treated with little respect by the Ibele people. Arrows were fired at them; Elisa was grabbed and thrown to the ground. While Danis held him with a spear at his throat, Bromley, sheltering behind a rock from flying arrows, talked fast. He persuaded the attackers that they had neither trade to steal, nor did they intend to harm the Danis. The tumult ebbed and the two men reached Hettigima two days later without further incident.

After Bromley left them, the party turned northwest, along a grassy ridge from where they could see the pyramid-shaped mountain at the junction of the Wolo and Baliem Rivers, the point at which they had chosen to cross the Baliem.

They crossed rolling country, pushed through knee-deep grass, trampled down high reeds, and often floundered waist deep through hidden pits of old village sites. The tracks crisscrossed, seeming to lead nowhere. They wandered for some time in a maze before finding a well-worn path, indicating people, which took them through dense forest and came out at a watchtower. Although they had been descending into the Baliem since early afternoon, they had seen no people.

Dawson went on ahead to set up camp, while Bond and Veldhuis climbed up over a ridge and down into the gardens on the other side to contact the people and to buy food. They found them here, many men and women, industriously digging potatoes. The two men stood in full view of the people, giving them time to adjust to their presence, but they were completely ignored. They called out again and again but with no response from the busy diggers. Confused, the two men, calling as they approached, went down the hill towards them. Suddenly they were seen. With a startled cry the gardeners grabbed their bags, scrambled over the far fence, fled through another garden and over another fence into the village. In a few minutes about forty armed men streamed out of the houses.

Gathering together, they crept along the fences until within about one hundred yards of Bond and Veldhuis. The body of warriors and the two lone, unarmed white men stood facing each other, neither knowing what to do.

Veldhuis and Bond held their empty hands high and called words of greeting and friendship. They asked for food and held up shell, but could not be sure that their words were understood. These people possibly spoke another dialect or even a different language from the people in the Ibele Valley.

Veldhuis and Bond moved towards them. The group moved back. The two men hesitated about going down toward them and the Danis felt the same way about coming up the hill.

"Well, here's a stalemate," said Bond and sat down. Veldhuis sat too.

"We'll try again," said Hans edging towards the group. With a rattle of arrows, they darted towards a clump of bamboo and waited. Veldhuis and Bond waited too and the crowd edged out from their shelter.

The men tried miming their hunger. They rubbed their stomachs and ate imaginary potatoes, holding out shell and red handkerchiefs towards the Danis. A man broke from the crowd, ran back to the village, and returned with two large cooked potatoes. Jubilant that they had put their message over, the men went down to meet him. That cut the fellow's nerve; he turned and sped back to the tensely waiting mob!

Realizing that the Dani must come his own way, Hans and

Russell sat down again holding out both hands—one empty and the other with shell in it.

In the same way, with hands extended, one holding the potatoes and the other to receive his pay, the Dani warily edged closer with fear in his eyes and his quivering body beaded with perspiration. The potatoes and shell were exchanged. The trader turned and darted back to the band whose intense gaze had not left his fearful approach to the unknown strangers. His friends crowded around, examining the shell. Its genuineness confirmed, they ran to the houses for more potatoes. Stabbing their spears into the ground, without hesitation they hurried to the men waiting on the hill. On receiving their shells and red handkerchiefs, they sealed the transactions with greasy bear hugs.

In a few Dani words and much sign language Veldhuis and Bond impressed upon the Danis that there were many hungry men over the hill, wanting potatoes. Soon hundreds of men, women, and children lined the fence which Dawson and the carriers had erected around the camp. None were armed, but they were bold and aggressive, pushing through the barricade, fingering and making off with utensils and equipment until strong measures had to be used to keep them beyond the fence.

That night, dark with thick cloud, the watch shouted into the tent. Veldhuis, awakened from sound sleep, shot up crying, "Oh, Lord, they've come! it's an attack." Flaying through a confusion of mosquito nets and sleeping bags, the men were outside in no time, questioning the guard.

"I saw a man crawling under the fence. I think that there are more with him, but when I shouted, they ran away," he answered.

The men beat around the camp but discovered no one. They laughed about their own startled confusion in the tent, but their ears strained for the sound of marauders and sleep did not come again.

5

The Last Stand Against Entry

THE NIGHT PASSED without further sign of prowlers. Anxious
to be away, they broke camp early. The worst of their journey
still lay ahead of them; they must cross the Baliem, enter the
Wolo Valley, and climb over Mud Pass at seventy-five hundred
feet. They knew that this day could be long and trying.

Although they had radio contact with the coast and three
rifles, which Dutch officialdom had insisted they carry, they
were well aware of how useless these would be in a sudden
attack or ambush. Their confidence was in the overshadowing
of the Lord. Therefore, having committed the day to Him,
they were away early—down the ridge and through the gardens
where they had encountered the heavy population the day
before.

Still high above the Baliem, they could see the approximate
direction of their path into the Wolo Valley. The rising sun
broke through the clouds, floodlighting the irregular limestone-
scarred mountains guarding the Wolo Valley in the north.

The Baliem Valley, slashed by the wide brown river which
they hoped to cross that day, stretched below them. Houses,
gardens, and long lines of fences sprawled over the grassy
slopes of the foothills and out onto the flat valley floor. Blue
smoke from domestic fires filtered through thatched roofs. The
rosy glow of sunrise faded, leaving the valley in somber grey
shadow. The carriers shivered and plunged on down the hill.

By noon they were down in the valley abreast of Pyramid
Rock rising perpendicularly for eight thousand feet out of flat
ground. From here they were to cross the valley to the junction
of the Baliem and Wolo rivers and follow the Wolo up into

the valley where it had its source. Rounding a spur, running out from the rock, they came to a village where the track which they had been following ended.

"Where is Wolo?" they asked the villagers. Although another path led off at right angles from the village the Danis pointed towards high wild sugarcane without any sign of a track. The men protested but the Danis insisted. Pushing into the cane, they beckoned to the men who, hesitant and dubious, had no alternative but to follow. Their fears increased when an excited band of young bloods dashed off on the other track. While their eyes and ears looked for any sign of ambush, their hearts sent out silent messages to God.

Without warning they plunged down into the mud and slush of deep drains interlacing an old garden site. As they floundered out, helpless and vulnerable to attack, their nerves strained to the breaking point.

The cane thickened and increased to twenty feet in height. The men hacked at it with their machetes but could cut only a narrow tunnel through the dense reed. The stench of stagnant mud and rotting grass hit their nostrils and sickened their stomachs. An eerie grey light filtering through the grass above their heads increased their sudden claustrophobia. They stifled a rising desire to rush at the cane, push it back, trample it down, and fight a way out. They inwardly fought to maintain calm, to encourage the line of sweating, frightened carriers, the trembling woman, and whimpering children. Convinced that an ambush had been planned, each man waited for a devilish war cry, flaying axes, and stabbing spears to break upon them as they stumbled into some trap.

After four hours of gruelling torture they suddenly emerged from the cane into a glade where two gnarled old men sat warming themselves by a fire. Ingratiating themselves to the trekkers with flattering embraces and sly pats, they invited them to sit at the fire. Veldhuis, tense and wary from the ordeal in the cane, pushed the old men aside and called to his line, "This is one place where we don't sit down," and marched them through the clearing.

Five minutes out of the glade they met the warriors who had run off at the entrance of the cane; they were formed up in rows before a platform. The Dani platoon called to the carrier line to halt. Certain that their intent was evil, the men refused to stop and pushed on towards the Baliem River.

BATTLE CRY. Wolo warriors charge into battle.

Two hundred armed and decorated warriors ran beside them, excitedly pushing and jostling the nerve-racked carriers. Nearing the Baliem the Danis formed themselves into an attacking square and rushed ahead, shouting and yelling wildly. Danis streamed down from the gardens on the Wolo valley side of the Baliem and massed on the opposite bank. Dancing up and down on their respective shores, brandishing spears, hurling insults and threats at each other, they warmed up for a foray, taking no notice of the strangers.

The missionaries had expected that the Baliem crossing would be difficult. They watched this wide, deep river rushing against boulders and tumbling debris over breaking rapids as it raced away to the east; and they knew that their ingenuity would be taxed to get the twenty adults, the children, and equipment over without separating the party.

Many fallen trees, dried out on the bank, enabled them to build a raft to cross the river. They chose a point where the current would carry the raft to the opposite bank. In two hours the raft was completed and loaded with the equipment, the family, two Sengge men, and Hans Veldhuis, who could not swim. Fred Dawson, a strong swimmer, volunteered to go over first, with the rope tied about his waist, and then pull the raft across. The rest were to swim with the logs, pushing them to the other bank. When Dawson had reached the other side and found himself a foothold, he shouted, "OK, ready! Let her go!"

The others shoved the laden raft into the water. The current caught at it and swung it downstream. From the opposite bank, Fred strained to pull it across, but it jerked at him, tore at his muscles, and pulled him into the chilly stream. Bond left the raft and swam across to hold the rope with Dawson. Juggling for a foothold, gasping for breath in the ice cold water, they could not shift the raft against the flow of the current. The carriers, swimming alongside, could do nothing to direct it. Sucked by the current it swung downstream, pulling Dawson and Bond into deep water. The two men strained at the rope, the water pulled against them, and the rope snapped like a thread. The freed raft spun forward, swirled around a bend and out of sight, with the carriers clinging desperately to it.

Dawson and Bond with their backs to the push of the main current clutched at a half-sunken tree trunk, twenty feet from the bank on the outside of a wide turn. The mountain water froze their breath and paralyzed their limbs. Knowing that his strength was gone, Dawson was reluctant to let the stump go and head for the bank.

The Baliem warriors, forgetting their war in the excitement

of the white men's activities, poked long poles towards the stranded men. Bond slid into the water and struck out for the poles. They tied cane to another pole, threw it to Dawson and pulled him ashore, too.

The two clambered up the ten-foot cliff and pushed their way down stream through trackless cane growing along the bank to discover what had happened to the others. They felt certain the raft had gone and their friends were drowned, that they were alone in the Baliem without food or equipment. A distant shout reached them. They rushed forward—at least someone was safe!

Some distance down the river, they found Veldhuis, the carriers, the raft, and all the equipment; and they could scarcely believe the miracle. The raft had bumped over snag, tilting it to one side and throwing off those who were clutching the upraised side. How they reached the shore, they were never quite certain, but cold and exhausted, they lay sprawled on the ground.

The Danis had rushed along the bank with the raft, thrusting out poles and vines to those on board, whose snatching hands missed the aid as the raft swept by. Someone had caught an overhanging branch and swung the raft far enough in for the Baliem men to grab it and heave it ashore.

Latent human kindness, smothered by superstitious fears and cruelty, now rose up in the primitive men. The party, blue and numb from cold and exhaustion, could not have resisted a Dani attack. Apathetically they watched the warriors carry up the miraculously preserved equipment and stack it carefully, making no attempt to steal. The Baliem men cleared the ground, put up the tents, and lit a fire by pulling string quickly across flint. The Wolo men shouted encouragement across the river. When they had finished their chores, the evening rains came and the Danis went to their villages.

After a miserable night the group moved upstream to a better campsite on a wide pebbly beach in a bend of the river. They made a couple of light rafts which would take three boys, but although easily handled, they were not adequate for the transportation of their equipment.

The Sengge men made their own concept of a raft suitable for the situation and fashioned paddles to propel it. Crossing, they were carried downstream. They turned and paddled hard upstream only to find themselves revolving in midstream. The Wolo men, not to be outdone in all this raftmaking activity, tied two small logs together and pushed out at a forty-five-degree angle across the river. Their adept handling of the crude little craft indicated that this was their usual mode of river crossing. They could not understand why the white man would not put his equipment on board.

Giving up hope of success with the rafts, the men radioed the Sentani base for the airplane to drop a rubber dinghy, rope, and food for the carriers. They prepared the Danis for the coming of the plane by pointing to the sky, flapping their arms, and dropping things onto the ground. The Danis nodded their heads, smiled, and imitated the missionaries. But, when the Sealander swooped in, they pushed their heads well down into anything that would hide them; bare, brown mounds protruding skywards identified their positions.

When they saw the dinghy inflated and the men and equipment taken safely across the river, they conceded that the white man was not quite so helpless as they had thought.

The men heaved up the bank, loaded on their packs and, pushed into the Wolo Valley with some apprehension. When the Wolo men had barred the path of the Archbold Expedition through here with some five hundred spearmen, Van Arken had used force, killing one Dani and wounding two. Questions nagged at the men. Would the Wolos resist again? Would they remember? Had the desire for revenge burned within them through the years? Would it flame into a vicious gory payback?—or could the party outwit them?

They walked through the valley not knowing whether the shadow of death hung over it.

"Well, all our fears were for nought," they congratulated

each other. "Van Arken's patrol must have really put some fear
into them. They know what a gun can do."

"See, there's not a weapon among them."

"Amazing, you know! We expected so much trouble here
and we're being treated better in this valley than anywhere
else—so far."

They camped on a gentle slope; below them the Wolo River
twisted and churned at the foot of massive mountains, until
it plunged into caves festooned with bats hanging asleep and
reappeared on the other side of the hills. That this unlikely
site would someday be the airstrip of the Wolo Mission Station did not suggest itself to the missionaries, who were at that
time without experience of highland air operation.

At sixty-five hundred feet, with sharp winds blowing from
the mountains rising another four thousand feet above them,
the carriers crouched at the blaze of a fire. They spread their
numbed fingers to it and let the heat burn their pinched faces
until they were red and dry.

They cooked sweet potatoes in the coals and ate them hot.
Warmed inside and out, their spirits rose and their strength
revived. To quench their thirst they bit into cucumbers, split-
ting them with a crack, and sucked the juice from the sugarcane that the Wolos had brought in great numbers in exchange
for cowrie shells. The ingratiating manners of both parties
made the transaction a bestowal of gifts and a pact of friendship; but greed flickered in the Wolos' eyes and burned in their
hearts. They planned to kill.

Tamene, a young war leader, felt an unusual interest stirring
in his heart at the presence of the white trekkers. His superstitious mind saw them as a good omen. While the trekkers,
ever alert but deceived by the Wolos' friendliness, chatted in
sign language with some of the great crowd that thronged the
camp, others planned their destruction. Tamene could not feel
happy about killing the white men. He sensed a hesitation in
some of the scheming killers and pleaded for their lives.

"I'll go to my village and get a pig for them," he declared.

"You empty-head! Don't give these fellows a pig—much better to kill them and take their things. We could do with a few of their knives and axes," the old man advised.

But Tamene went to get the pig, and while the would-be killers hesitated, the trekkers moved on.

Years later, sitting on Russell Bond's home built almost on that same campsite, Tamene told his experiences of the night the men came through his valley. Bond had not remembered Tamene, but God had chosen His man and had kept His own from savagery.

A young lad from the next valley sold them a pig which they roasted and ate in no-man's-land. Fortified, they pushed on into the main Ilugwa Valley. The usual host of screaming, armed, grease-smeared Danis streamed out to intercept and challenge their approach. The upward thrust of their nasal pig tusks, a sign that an enemy was to be engaged, warned the missionaries to be prudent.

That night they camped at the edge of the bush near the pass. Shells were given and an axe formally presented to the chief, splendidly decorated with the cockatoo feathers of his office.

Next morning they climbed a small knoll and started up a track which disappeared into the bush. The men followed this track for four hours while natives hooted and shouted around them, brandishing spears and gesticulating frantically as though trying to prevent them. Tense and strained from the continual prodding of excited armed men from behind, the rearguard changed frequently.

An hour's vigorous climbing the following day brought them to the top of a ridge falling away into a deep valley. The long rays of morning sunshine lit up the eight-thousand-foot, wind-sculptured mountain range beyond and cast dark shade in the valley. Two sentinel peaks guarded Mud Pass which they must cross to enter into the Hablifoerie Valley. Morning mists lay still and white in shadowed pockets. Blue smoke, seeping through village roofs, spiralled upright in the windless air.

The trekkers heaved on their pack harnesses and lifted the loads which felt heavier each weary day. The road ahead would be the hardest walking yet.

The track which they had been following forked; they deliberated and chose the one that had been most used which led diagonally across the ridge. By noon this trail vanished into impenetrable jungle. The men returned to the ridge and followed the other path, which led down into the valley. This too disappeared into the bush. The men were confused. Van Arken's report of the Archbold Expedition had indicated that here his patrol had passed through a heavily populated area.

Again, they retraced their steps. Bond and Veldhuis, leaving Dawson alone with the carriers and equipment, returned to the Ilugwa. After much palavering, they managed to persuade some Danis to come and guide them. Immediately, these felfellows plunged into the bush and hacked a way through scrub, fern, and secondary growth. Bewildered, the men followed; but soon they realized from the overgrown drains that this was an abandoned village site, and the heavily populated area of which Van Arken had written. Old scars cut into trees at a certain place indicated that the Archbold patrol had been through here.

By three in the afternoon the UFM party had cut its way, foot by foot, to the Idaab River and entered dense, pathless rain forest. The guides had reached their limit. Refusing all offers they returned to their own village. Left to themselves the men worked on a northeasterly compass course towards Mud Pass, taking their bearings from the Idaab River which they knew fell to the south. Three different routes took them nowhere.

The next day they tried another three routes, but could not find a way through the tall timber cluttered with undergrowth and vines and dripping with moisture. After they had spent three hours in frustrated effort, a couple of Ilugwa men appeared from nowhere. When they offered to guide the patrol to the Pass, the lost men knew that God had indeed sent them. They led off with confidence straight into the trackless, impossible jungle. The dense trees rising to two or three hundred feet hid the contour of the ground. The party judged that they were following along a shoulder with slightly rising ground on either side of them. They left a creek behind and crossed over the top of the shoulder. A spring oozed out of the ground and trickled away from them. They were through the Pass. Alone, they could have found it only by chance.

The guides returned home, leaving them alone once more with their compasses and the trackless forest.

The Danis of the Ilugwa Valley had sold them no food and it was obvious that there would be no more villages until they entered the Hablifoerie. They radioed Sentani to replenish their exhausted supplies with an airdrop.

It had taken them hours to fell the tall timbers, to clear enough space to erect tents on the thick moss-covered ground at seventy-five hundred feet on the top of Mud Pass. Now they had to begin again to clear for an airdrop.

They were out of food two days before they had opened an area large enough for the airplane to operate over.

The natural cloud barrier on the surrounding high peaks caused frequent heavy rains. The dark, fetid gloom of the fog-shrouded forest, the dripping trees, the spongy moss into which at times they sank to their knees, constant hunger and weariness depressed them almost to despair.

The Sengge boys, children of the tropics, sat like zombies on the top of their island world. This was a country they didn't know and didn't understand. It filled them with superstitious terror of the unknown. They sat immobile, vacant-eyed with open mouths. Their fatalistic minds recognized only the end. They could not be roused to perform any of the routine camp chores or to prepare for the expected aircraft.

The missionaries themselves worked alone. They too were anxious almost to sickness. The possibility that their bivouac, a dot in the thick limitless jungle, would be unsighted by the Sealander gnawed at them. The attitude of the carriers left them in no doubt of the problems that they would have should that happen. Tensions strained at their tempers. Constant

vigil guarded against internal strife, but natural weaknesses
caught them too often.

Each morning they lit wet wood with kerosene and tried
to put warmth and enthusiasm into their cold and miserable
bodies from the smoky half-hearted fire.

They had searched for five hours for enough burnable wood
to build a large signal fire.

Twelve bags were dropped. Of these only four were recovered, and one was a box of heavy knives and trade goods,
useless until they reached the Hablifoerie. The men were
sorely disappointed. Their spirits were too low to be encouraged by the fact that a third of a drop was a good recovery
under almost impossible conditions.

Fifty-five hundred feet below them lay the Hablifoerie River.
They slashed a compass trail through the bush. It led onto a
rock ledge jutting out into space. They stood still, awed by
the majestic vastness of mountain ridge after ridge—wooded,
grassed, rock-faced, red, green, and glinting limestone. The
spirit of the country, a formidable presence, breathed upon
them.

Surely to every explorer who views the land he has conquered comes a surge of ownership. From the writhing river
in the canyon below to the billowing snow white clouds on the
purple distant horizon, they could stretch out a hand and say,
"Today you are ours. Today we have conquered you. Tomorrow God shall dwell with you." Hope had drawn back the
curtain to show the despairing men the promise of a beyond.

They turned from the ledge. They had not conquered yet.
Hordes of spear-brandishing warriors, holding loosely their
passions, were behind them. Before them—dense jungle, sheer
precipice, and deep ravine. One slip and New Guinea would
yet dash another intruder to his death. Although they had
feared the reactions of natives, they were very dependent upon
their help.

They returned to the top of the pass. Abandoning the compass, Veldhuis, Bond, and some carriers followed a stream to
find a way down into the valley, again leaving Dawson and a

few carriers with the equipment. A party of mean fellows, evidently intent on mischief, came around the camp. All day they harried the waiting men, attempting to steal and threatening violence. When the successful survey party returned, Dawson and the carriers were exhausted from the strain and the miserable climate.

After another cold night in the mist and fog, under dripping trees in damp clothes and bedding, the patrol started the almost perpendicular descent. They had broken camp so often that the spice of adventure had completely gone. They seemed to be shutting fog into their packs. The soggy tent now weighed a good eighty pounds.

Halfway down they slipped and stumbled for a foothold, through greasy, treacherous shale from a landslide.

"Look, the lake! The lake!" someone cried. Its sunlit water flickered through the trees. The end was near. They gazed in silence—would they make it that far?

Someone said, "When I get down there and throw off this pack, will I ever put my feet up!"

In a few days they would pitch a permanent camp. They felt that they were coming home.

As they descended the air grew warmer. The Sengge men recognized familiar flora and the tracks of pig and cassowary. Their spirits rose and tensions relaxed. They were in country which they understood, and free from harrying strangers.

Van Arken's map showed a track right down the mountain, but there was no track and no people. Again the Danis' semi-nomadic habits had taken them elsewhere. The men picked up a stream at the bottom of the ridge which corresponded with one on the map and followed it right down to the Hablifoerie River.

Their spirits were high as they pitched camp. They had come all the way down the mountain without accident. They had only to cross the Hablifoerie and the next day they would be at the lake. They slept, lulled by the perpetual roar of the river's tumbling water.

In the morning they examined the river, hoping to cross at

that point. Its boiling flood waters, churning and roaring like a maddened beast, indicated that there was no alternative but to follow the route which the Dutch party had taken and cross two hours downstream.

Here at the downstream crossing the three-hundred-foot width of the Hablifoerie narrowed to ten. The pent-up water, thundering with rage, hurled itself through the restricting chasm. With dismay, the men viewed the precipitous cliffs rising from the river. The south bank dropped steeply to a rock ledge. A flimsy bridge of saplings lashed with cane rested one end onto the rock ledge; the other butted into the sheer rock face of the northern wall. Although the bridge looked rotten and unsafe, fresh tracks encouraged the men to accept it as the crossing used by the Papuans. But they also knew that with their hiking boots and heavy packs, they could not match the highland New Guineans for agility and surefootedness.

Cautiously, they lowered themselves over the edge of the cliff. Jagged rocks, like bayonets guarding a prohibited crossing, resisted their advance. Gently they edged from the narrow ledge onto the rickety bridge, which at close quarters was more rotten than they had feared.

Each man eased himself to his hands and knees. He was now face to face with the tumult seething below. The moisture-heavy packs piled on their backs lessened their sense of balance. Inch by agonizing inch, they pulled themselves across the swaying bridge, willing themselves to keep their eyes fixed to the two-foot limit of frail logs, fighting inward panic and dizziness.

The mother and father each carried a clinging child and anxiously crawled the rotting saplings. The man with the eighty-pound tent crouched to his knees. The load swayed. The men caught their breath. Each man took his turn, while the others waited, willing him to safety. Too tense to pray and nauseated to the pits of their stomachs, their eyes were drawn as though by a magnet. They were part of him in his torment.

Across the chasm they cautiously crept, their searching fingers testing and grasping jutting rocks. Slowly they pulled themselves from one marginal foothold to the next, up and up to the rim of the precipice. They relaxed. Tension seeped out, weakness and fatigue came heavily upon them.

"Surely, that's the last stand against our entry," they encouraged each other. "We should come out to the lake soon."

"Half an hour down the bank from the crossing, according to Van Arken," maintained Veldhuis, who was relying on his memory of the lieutenant's report.

With eager anticipation they lumbered wearily along the riverbank on the last leg of their trek. Half an hour passed with no sign of the lake or the creek running out from it. An hour, and the men's anxiety mounted. Another fifteen minutes, and still not a trace of the lake and its outlet.

"Surely we've missed it somewhere," they agreed. They retraced their dragging steps to the river crossing. Opposite the bridge there appeared to be a knoll which the desperate men thought they could circumvent to the lake on the other side. The hill was not a knoll, but the spur of a main ridge with no way round it. The men were completely lost. Disappointed, discouraged, and hungry they pitched camp in heavy rain and semidarkness. They had planned an airdrop to time with their arrival at the lake, and had skimped their meager rations. Now they were gone. The carriers scrounged in the bush for leaves and berries, which staved the hunger pains but did not lift their spirits.

Reluctantly, they radioed Sentani for another drop. They had hoped to spare the carriers this extra load. A cracked tail wheel delayed the Sealander another two days. Apart from the berries and leaves gathered from the bush, they were entirely out of food.

Scouting parties searched for the lake but it was completely hidden. Was New Guinea tantalizing them in a malicious game? They built two huge fires at both ends of the area cleared for dropping and tuned their radio to follow the Sealander's flight. Heavy overcast all the way in from Sentani threatened to force back the plane. The pilot probed into the clouds, searching for an opening. He found one just above the lake and their campsite; it was large enough for the drop. Every sack but one was recovered.

"Only this mountain lies between you and the lake. Three to five trekking miles should take you there," the pilot called through the plane's radio. Then, after giving them an exact compass direction to the lake, he headed back to the coast.

Hans Veldhuis' misreading of half an hour for two hours in Van Arken's report had cost the party another uncomfortable week on the trail.

Ten minutes out of camp, the party who went to cut a trail over the three thousand foot mountain stumbled upon the lost sack for which they had vainly searched in the thick undergrowth the previous day. In five and a half hours they had cut a path to the top. The next day they cut through to the lake.

The path to their goal lay wide open before them. They spent Sunday in camp resting. During the month they had faced death almost daily in numerous ways. There had been no loss, no sickness, no accident, no cowardice. Often they had been depressed, lonely, discouraged, and afraid. They had made mistakes. There is no shame in these—only in the weakness of giving way.

Each man knew well his own limitations, but God had taken what had been made available to Him and lifted it above the ordinary. They were men sent by God to "make straight the way of the Lord."

6

An Airstrip for Cowrie Shells

THE SURVEY PATROL through to Lake Archbold had initiated the missionaries into the ruggedness of the terrain and the unpredictability of its energetic people. During the eighteen months that followed, the little settlement at Lake Archbold, its supply line kept open by the *Pathfinder*, became a base. From here friendly contacts with the people were made, and the land was further surveyed. On one such trek, southwest of Archbold, two new recruits, Bert Power and Ross Bartel, with four Sengge men climbed the adjoining ridges and visited the villages clinging to them. Danis who had been down to the lake welcomed them fervently and introduced them to friends.

They slept one night high up near the top of a ridge. People came crowding from up and down the mountains, bringing gifts and receiving medicine. They pointed out areas and groups of people, including their enemies, in the far distance.

Next morning the party passed over the top of the main ridge and went down to a cluster of villages in a small valley. They glimpsed a strip-site that had been seen on a previous air survey. The next day they persuaded the headman, a fellow with black, greasy hair hanging to his thighs, to take them down to have a look at it. At first he had argued that it was hostile territory, but the sight of promised cowrie shells overcame his fear of the enemy.

By noon they were on a high ridge overlooking the Bokondini Valley. Below them stretched three flat, grassy airstrip sites. The northern, eastern, and western walls of the valley were crowded with huts, clinging to the crags. Down in that valley were men who needed God, and they needed missionaries to teach them.

Back at the lake the men told what they had seen. For days the missionary conversation centered around the valley over the ridge. They were convinced that in order to reach these people effectively they must go in and live with them.

Charles Horne, a Queenslander who at that time, 1956, had spent fifteen years on the Fly River with the UFM and another two at Tari in the Papuan Southern Highlands, came in to lead the West New Guinea program.

In mid-February he visited Lake Archbold for a conference, prior to his family's permanent move west. With Hans Veldhuis he flew in over the Wolo Valley and marked it for a station with expansion towards the Ilugwa.

From the Wolo Valley they climbed back over the Baliem divide, saw a considerable population on the northern slopes, and came down into the Hablifoerie River system to the proposed Bokondini airstrip site which Bert Power had seen from the ridge southwest of Archbold. Flying with wheels a few feet above the high sloping plateau, they skimmed the six hundred yards of almost natural strip. At the western end a grassy knoll limited the airfield to a one-way approach and takeoff. The opposite end fell to a thousand foot chasm, giving clearance from the seven thousand foot mountain range on the north side.

The Australian Baptist Missionary Society and the Regions Beyond Missionary Union had men at Sentani looking for a way into the interior. A conference with these men produced the decision for them to join with the UFM party, walk in from Lake Archbold to Bokondini, help to build the strip, and then use it as their jumping off base—the Baptists to the North Baliem and the RBMU to the Swart Valley.

On the last day of April, towards the end of the "Wet," the party with several Sengge men and led by Bert Power, left Archbold and came to the bank of the flooded Hablifoerie. They chopped a tree, two hundred feet in height, to fall across the river to make a bridge over which to carry their radio and packs. Its branches fell into the water. The current swung the trunk around and downstream. They lost their bridge. Next they tried a jungle bridge of vine. With no tree stumps suitably placed on either bank for securing the cane, each attempt failed. They resorted to the rubber dinghy but the current flipped it over.

While walking towards the north, still searching for a crossing, one of the two men shouted, "Look at that Dani! He's wading across the river. Here we've been trying to find a way to the other side and that fellow simply walks across!"

The men collected their gear and waded in, following the sandbar known to the local people. After two days of fruitless effort, they had made it across in several minutes. On the southern side they floundered, sometimes chest deep, through miry swamp before they reached rising ground.

At the village of Umaga, two hours out of Bokondini, the carriers dropped their packs, refusing to cross the frontier into enemy territory.

The Dani tribe, stretching from the eastern limits of the Baliem to the Ilago Valley in the west, is divided into two large dialectical groups, with slight changes in the spread away from the center. Within each group are hundreds of units identified by their locality and clan names. Interclan fighting takes place among these. Friendly groups confederate against common enemies. Clans centered around a paternal leader live in small hamlets. Each hamlet has one large men's house, where brothers, sons, and nephews of the headman sleep and eat. Their wives live with the pigs in smaller houses on either side of this central house, forming a large horseshoe.

When the carriers threw down their loads at Umaga, old Mabu, the paternal head, pressed the party to remain.

"You must live with us," he said. Then, turning to his village men, commanded, "Don't you carry for them. We shall build them a house and they will live with us."

"But," protested the missionaries, "we must go on down there to the flat ground so that we can build an airstrip on which the plane can land."

When Mabu further restrained his followers, Power showed
them cowrie shells. Avarice lit their eyes and deafened their
ears to their chief's orders. Shoving others aside, they snatched
at the missionaries' gear. A leader, dubbed "General Mac" by
the trekkers, emerged and formed the successful grabbers and
the empty-handed, greedy for a likely handout, into a close
mass. With much yelling, yodelling, and exuberance, they
ran in a tight circle. Suddenly a man broke from the group.
The others, still running and chanting, followed him, bunching
again in a solid body. They repeated this several times, then
wheeled and dashed off towards Bokondini. This exercise, the
missionaries were to learn, was their general preactivity pattern
for acquiring strength, whether for fighting, fence-building, or
feast-making. Later it prefaced their church attendance!

That evening when cool shadows lingered in the valley and
the women with string bags filled for the evening cooking, came
up out of the potato gardens, the missionaries climbed over
the brow of the hill into Bokondini.

The Dani men sent the women scurrying away, "Don't come
out! Are these spirit men or cannibals?"

They could relate the unknown and foreign only to their own
culture. These men came from over the ranges, therefore they
could be cannibals; but because they were white, they must
be spirits.

Axes and shell came out of the belly of that "wurra-wurra"
thing in which they travelled. Surely the mother of steel and
shell lived out there in Hollandia from where the airplane
came.

These men talked into boxes called radios to the spirits of
their ancestors, and their fathers' voices came back for all to
hear. When they asked, their ancestors sent food, axes, and
knives. Maybe they were spirit mediums used for the distri-
bution of shell and steel to the Danis. It was well to keep in
with these fellows.

Yet, the white men had those cameras, little things with the
big round eye through which they looked. Were they looking
right through a man's flesh to see his spirit, or were they look-

ing through a woman's skirt to see her nakedness? It was well for the women to keep away from them.

Conjecture became fact which they wove into their religious background. They were afraid, not knowing whether the intention of the white man towards them was for good or evil.

Hordes of Danis from the hamlets high in the ridges, deep in the valleys, and from way down the river came to the missionaries' camp, as though hypnotically drawn. Fear was in their eyes. They looked steadily back at the strangers before them, trying to anticipate their moves, assessing their thoughts and motives. Fear quivered on their lips and agitated the fingers on the bow strings.

The Danis felt it provident to satiate these possible cannibals and showered them with gifts of pork. A little fellow, his eyes wide and dark with terror, came to offer the visitors a baked potato. They ruffled his hair and patted his shoulder, trying to dispel the fear which prompted the gift of friendship.

Bert Power gave shells to the men whom he judged to be chiefs and waved aside those, who in hope of a gift, masqueraded as such. Later, familiarity confirmed the accuracy of his judgment.

"What's your name?" Power asked a lad in his early teens.

"Mut-mut."

"And what's yours?" he asked the boy's companion.

"Mit-mit."

"Mit-mit and Mut-mut! Are these your true names?" The boys shrugged and grinned, "Yes, our true names." But they had given false names lest, by giving the true, they put their spirits into the power of another for evil.

One night Bert Power was awakened by urgent whispering from outside the camp door.

"Tuan, Tuan, come here." ("Tuan" means "sir," although the Danis apply it to anyone "from the outside.")

Going out, he saw a fellow whom they had nicknamed "Slimy Slim."

"Whatever do you want at this hour of the night?"

"Tuan, are you a man with a body just like ours, or are you

a spirit? I want to feel your body to see if it is the same as a Dani body."

Power let him feel that he too was a man such as themselves.

Another old man, Topaga, made bold to confront the missionaries, demanding that they declare their purpose.

"Why have you come? Do you intend to kill and eat us? Will you live here for all time?"

The missionaries gave an honest answer.

"We have come to tell you about God who made all things good. We've come to do His work, to help you, to teach you, and heal your sick."

The old man shook his head and whistled against a finger knuckle bent in his mouth.

"Why should you come to help us for no gain to yourselves?"

He was still a little suspicious, but believed that they spoke the truth about curing the infirm. On the testimony of one of their men, Lobak, who had been down to the lake and seen the healing, the Bokondini people brought in their sick, carrying some on stretchers for miles over the mountains. Others had traveled from as far as Wolo and the Pyramid rock.

A Kelila man had come with yaws covering his back, chest, and head, and with one eye eaten away. Injections of penicillin cleared his infection.

While hunting in the bushland, a wild boar had ripped Kaniaganak's leg, laying it open to the bone. Shocked and bleeding, he was left alone in the rain on the cold of the mountainside.

"He mustn't have a fire or the spirits will see the light and come to torment him," his people explained. "Neither must he come to the village or the demons will enter the torn flesh. Then it will become putrid and he'll die."

Had the filth of the village infected the wound, then their prognosis would surely have transpired. Superstition provided their only understanding of the natural laws of disease and infection.

The missionaries found Kaniaganak, dressed the injury, and brought him to their house. Because of the fear of the spirits he refused to sleep anywhere near fire or light, but accepted the warmth of a blanket.

On another day Danis came running into the yard.

"Tuan, Tuan, bring your needle and come quickly, a woman has fallen on a fence and torn her stomach open."

When the missionaries arrived, the necessary operation had already been performed. The intestines had been rammed back and the flesh sutured with a thorn for a needle and bark for thread.

The Tuan gave her a shot of antibiotics and poured an antiseptic over the wound, feeling it was best to leave their surgery untouched.

A few days later he returned to see the patient but the hut was empty.

"Where's the woman with the stomach wound?" he asked a bystander.

The Dani jerked his head. "That's her working in the garden." The amazing effect of antibiotics on a people previously untouched by them, coupled with their native stoicism, worked miracles.

A mother brought her albino son from across the gorge. He was shockingly burnt on every part of his body from continual exposure to the sun.

"Would the missionary please give him an injection to make his tender white skin black and strong?"

But the missionary could only give clothing to protect him from the burning rays.

Men brought their sterile wives for an injection for fertility, only to discover that there were limits to the white man's "magic needle."

Daily, hundreds more than could be employed came to work on the airstrip for the coveted cowrie shells. At the end of the day these nonworkers cunningly joined the pay line. To keep tally of the employees a metal disc was given to each in the morning. When a worker returned his disc in the evening he received his wages. Boulders were dynamited and hauled to the sides, holes were filled, topsoil removed and the surface

SURVEY FOR AN AIRSTRIP. In the Baliem Valley, missionaries look over the terrain.

hardened. In ten days enough of the strip was surfaced to
take limited aircraft operations. With the opening of the Bokondini strip, the mission to the Danis was really initiated,
and the missionaries could settle down to learn more of the
Dani ways.

"Ndini," the flat ground where the air field was built, on the
shelf of the thousand-foot precipice above the Boko river—
hence Bokondini—was the traditional fighting and ceremonial
dancing ground of the people.

During one workday painted warriors came prancing and
shouting onto the flat ground to do battle with another group
who were advancing from the other end. Work progress waned
as the gangers cheered and incited their chosen side. The missionaries felt none too safe from the flying arrows and swinging
war axes.

Power approached the chief.

"Would it make any difference to you if you took your men off to the village to fight, as all this rather holds up our work?"

Philosophically the "generals" led their men to a more convenient place. War is not waged to gain territory but to raise the status of the leader and to demonstrate the prowess of the warriors. Battle is a religious rite.

In raids they looted enemy villages, burned houses, and left the earth scorched and desolate. Women and children, the aged and infirm were not spared in this crazed plunder of villages weakened under attack. In every group, many males in the pride of manhood between sixteen and thirty years were killed while fighting each year.

Boys, born into an atmosphere of war, spontaneously played at battles. When a youth was initiated into the tribal secrets of his manhood, it was drummed into him that he was a member of a group with ceremonial obligations and a duty to fight against a common enemy. He dared not neglect this debt inherited from his ancestors lest he invoke the wrath of their spirits. He was haunted by the fear that if he did not fight, he would not only become a nonentity but would be smitten with blindness. Although a warrior was striving for individual prowess, the survival of the group was also his objective.

War was the foundation of their religious system. Souvenirs taken from the enemy dead in battle became fetishes of importance in their animistic ceremonies. Although personally owned, they held communal significance in group ritualism. The position of a man's sacred stone, kept in a cupboard in a men's house, recorded his place in prebattle formation, what portion of pork he would eat at a ceremony, and what part he would take in tribal rites.

Consecration of fetishes gave battle strength. Observation of food taboos protected life in battle. Sacred objects, consecrated to give individual clan protection against sickness, were directed against the enemy to his detriment and their success in battle.

The most important Dani ceremonies were victory dances of religious significance. To abolish war would be to shake the

foundations of the tribe's religious system. It would mean a
total collapse and demoralization of the community unless it
was replaced by a religion that centered on pàcification. Only
the Christian religion with its foundation of "peace and goodwill toward men" could supersede this element so deeply em-
bedded in the Dani culture.

At first the Ndingguns, on the eastern ridge of the valley,
came to work on the airstrip alongside the Bokondinis. Then,
in the cold murkiness of an early dawn a band of their fighting
men sneaked into a sleeping Bokondini village, creeping close
to the silent huts.

A Ndinggun shouted and the rest took up the cry, "The
Ndingguns! The Ndingguns have come. War! War!"

Dazed by sleep and thinking the cry an alarm given by their
own people, each Bokondini warrior grabbed his weapons and
dashed through the doorway to have his head cleaved in two
by a waiting Ndinggun ax. Screaming with terror the nonfighters cringed back into the huts. The Ndingguns running from
house to house with burning faggots set light to the thatched
roofs. With a fierce roar, blood-red flames leapt skywards.
Chased by the inferno, the victims rushed outside in a blind
bid to escape through the enemy arrows. A deliberate arrow
pinned a baby to its mother's breast as she fled in terror.

The screams of the pursued ebbed away as they escaped
through the bush. With vicious yells the victors looted the
remaining huts, dispatched the dying, and barbarously butchered their bodies, throwing them to the pigs in a final gesture
of contempt.

The following night the Bokondinis retaliated to even the
score. In the morning they returned triumphant. "We've
killed nine and two more will die."

It didn't matter that some of the victims were old women
and little children. The count was even—eleven on each side.

When the Ndingguns and Bokondinis declared open war,
the Kambos from Kelila confederated with the Ndingguns.
This made a no-man's-land of the site where the missionaries
had established their camp. Every day befeathered sentries,

silhouetted against the blue sky, watched from the hill for an unaccounted figure or movement. In the mornings, before the work force came out, scouts beat along the creek bed and fences, and searched the wooded areas for sneaking raiders.

Without police organization, feuds savage as war were the tribe's only means of maintaining "law." The rule of might settled a dispute, deterred the adulterer, thief, rapist, or sorcerer. Therefore, an interhamlet feud often developed into bloody butchery.

Kuwalik saw an eagle building high in the boughs of a tree. He cut his mark into the trunk. All who passed by knew that when the three eggs hatched, Kuwalik would claim the fledglings. Checking on progress, his anger rose when he found the nest empty. He suspected Agagenak had stolen them and strode up to his village. Seeing the man outside his house he pulled his bow string, sending his arrow into Agagenak's chest. The valley rose in a furore. By evening houses were burnt, four men killed, and two wounded.

The lives of four men for the price of three bird's eggs! In the economy of the Dani culture, human life was more expendable than the right of the group.

7

Witches and Brides

THE AIR FILLED with staccato cries of hate and scorn. In the midst of a mob stood a woman, naked and unprotected, her body torn and bleeding. The pack had dragged her by the hair over stones and bush, and now they forced her to walk in her shame through the villages. Men and women spat at her, beat her with sticks, prodded her with spears, and slapped at her face with their bare hands. All the while they poured out venom in the foulest obscenities that their unenlightened minds could imagine. Terror and defiance fought together in her face.

"Kill her, kill her! She's a sorceress. She killed Apgwok with her magic. By her own tongue she said she bewitched him. Kill her! Kill her!"

Her sons too spat at her. Although she was their mother, she had become by her magic a hated member of society. She was no longer their mother to receive their affection but a menace to the group. She would die for her evil, but first they would vent their animosity against her.

The women held the secrets of sorcery. To them was given the power of the evil eye. Time revealed that there was no potency in the secretly guarded bits of moss, glistening quartz stone, little pieces of this and that which held some mystery or significance to the women who found and hoarded it against the day of its usefulness. An empty penicillin bottle thrown out by the missionary became an important medium in a sorceress' equipment. Maybe she thought some of its potency would be transmitted through her magic rites.

The real power of the sorcery was in the fear it produced in the men. In their thinking, no death or sickness came by any other cause than that of the women's witchcraft. Even death in battle had its primary cause in magic. The women had absolute power over the men in this thing. Any man against whom the magic had been directed was reduced to a despicable object of craven fear. Some, assuming that there was no relief from the curse, lay down, refused to eat, and died—as a direct result of suggestion. Others put up a fight to live.

The son of a powerful chief lost his foothold on a precipice and fell to the bottom, dashing his head against a stone. He died soon after. The howl of death lacerated the quietness of village domesticity, and the hunt for the sorceress began.

Bokowarek, the dead man's brother, was convinced that the curse was directed against the family and that he was to be the next victim. To persuade the powerful spirit Monggat to counteract any curse on his behalf, his clanswomen poured the blood of sacrificed pigs over his head and rubbed it into his face. The hot sticky fluid ran down his body, forming a pool around him. Voracious for relief from his fear, he scooped it up in his hands and drank, willing it to be effective.

When his entreaties and offerings were unavailing, Bokowarek turned to the white man's hypodermic needle to ward off the evil. To avoid the malevolent women, he crawled in the night through the long grass to the missionaries, who told him that there was no such medicine, but that faith in the Lord Jesus Christ could dispel his fear and give him hope and peace of heart. Bokowarek, not yet ready to put his trust in God, spent the day locked in the missionaries' woodshed, and then, when night came again, crept secretly home.

Several women had been named as the killer of the chief's son. To find the real culprit, men held a divination ceremony. Having killed a pig, they allotted portions of the flesh to the suspect women. Lighting a huge fire, they placed the meat at supposedly equal distances around it. As the fire blazed with searing heat, the men watched eagle-eyed to see whose piece of meat scorched. The owner of the singed meat was pronounced the culprit. To confirm the woman's guilt, they split the lobe of her ear. When the blood flowed, there was no doubt of her crime. The men drew their bows in hate and arrowed her where she stood.

In a culture centered in spirit worship, evil spirits periodically inhabited the worshippers, especially those who acted as mediums on their behalf. The women were naturally modest, but the coarse obscenities to which some gave themselves could have stemmed only from an actual spirit of lust. Such spirits of hate, anger, and fear forced their victims to acts of violence beyond their control. For some, both men and women, the rigors of the culture were too much, and minds gave away under the strain. Madness was common and the community unprotected.

Brides were purchased with pigs, special cream cowrie shells with four bumps, and the green, polished spirit stones, worth a month's wages and quarried from the cliffs to the west. A man of property could afford more than one wife. Old Yukwanak, the chief, was well established with ten wives and numerous heirs.

With the paying of the bride price, the woman belonged exclusively to one man who became responsible to house and protect her. He cleared and fenced the garden areas, while she tended the crops and the swine, and bore children. If a wife left her husband, her family was obliged to return the price. When a man seduced another's wife, he became responsible for compensation to the woman's family and answerable to the irate husband. He was also compelled to reimburse the family of a neglected wife.

Because the paying of the bride price in full spread over a long period, sometimes several years after the ceremony, a broken contract involved many in a group, and frequently resulted in bitter dispute and bloodshed. The method of bride payment deterred loose living and prevented a man from merely purchasing a wife without moral obligations.

On the first day of the wedding ceremony, covering three but not necessarily consecutive days, a feast for the bride-

groom's preparation was held at his village. Contributions to
the bride were finalized at this time.

The next part of the ceremony, "the catching of the bride"
took place at the bride's hamlet the following day or even several days later. The bride hid, usually in an obvious place, and
was found by her brother who slung her over his shoulder
and carried her off, kicking and screaming, to be dressed for
her wedding. Some young brides were serious in their ob-
jections, but most came willingly, while feigning violent protest
as a display of maidenly virtue.

With her arms supported head high on a sapling suspended
between two posts, the bride stood for several hours while
women relations wound yards of braided colored cord around
her thighs into a roll about six inches thick. String bags, dyed
with red ochre, were hung over her head, falling to the back
of her knees.

Although women left their breasts uncovered, it was in-
decorous to leave the buttocks bare. While the bride was
dressing, the pigs had been killed and some of the entrails tied
around the girl's arm to promote fertility. When the pigs were
cooked and carved, the bride distributed the meat, giving the
largest and fattest portions to the most important guests.

On the third day the bride and her attendants went to her
husband's village. Here they ate another feast, haggled over
the price, and received the first installment of the bride price.

The missionaries' initial approach to a new society is to win
its confidence. Barriers of suspicion and language prevent
ready familiarization with native custom. Therefore, the missionary moves cautiously into ceremonies and entertainments in
an unknown culture lest he offend or is himself embarrassed.
Because no primitive culture has a festivity without religious
significance, the missionaries to Bokondini made a practice
of not attending any function without an invitation.

Courting was not a strictly private pastime, but a group
affair where youths and maidens gathered together, passed arm
bands, and sang until inhibitions were lowered and license began. The first party of missionaries to Bokondini used to wander

over to the hut and watch the young Danis singing for an hour
or so without discovering the real import of the occasion, although dubious of its outcome.

One afternoon the boys came to Bert Power. "Tuan, you
come and sing with us tonight."

"Is this singing good or bad?"

"Oh, it's very good," the lads assured him. "All right. I'll
bring some of the Sengge boys with me, too," said Power,
wanting to identify himself with these people, but wary of
their classification of good.

He sat with a group of boys, and the singing and the ex-
changing began.

Power detected a change in the singing as the boys and girls
began to shift their positions. Then he found himself between
two girls. Somebody put the fire out. His suspicions were
confirmed when the girls giggled and squealed.

"Here, blow that fire up!" he shouted. "What's going on
here?"

"Tuan, this is no good," affirmed the Sengge lads.

Power stood up, "Right, I'm going home and you boys are
coming with me."

And they went home, leaving the girls sitting alone.

The Australian missionaries had postponed their own marriages, left familiar friendships, and given up the security and
prospects of remunerative positions for no other motive than
that of bringing to the Stone Age Danis life in Jesus Christ.
They used every opportunity to show them the love and righteousness of God. Easing the Papuan's misery where possible,
they made no attempt to introduce a Western civilization.
They aimed to so present Christ that the people would accept
Him and make Him the pivot of their lives. Any cultural
changes would then be direct results of lives transformed
through Him. Seed planted would bear indigenous fruit.

The Danis were entirely unaware that there was any life
different from theirs. As far as they knew, they were the sole
inhabitants of the earth, apart from a few insignificant "cannibals" over the ranges. Anything outside their knowledge was

mythical. While considering themselves the supreme beings, they were nevertheless conscious of these three basic needs: health, food, and eternal life. Acquisition of the same could only come by the pacification of vindictive spirits through obedience to their cruel demands.

Although the missionaries knew that the Danis had no hope of eternal life, they were ignorant at that time of the myth of their loss of eternal life and their forlorn hope of its recovery. But they saw the Papuans' need in sickness and won their confidence with the healing of their hypodermic syringe.

Aware that the Danis' interest in them was becoming increasingly materialistic, the missionaries persisted in persuading the people of their philanthropy and winning their regard by helping them in their husbandry. The Danis were agriculturists growing sweet potatoes for the basic crop, as well as bananas, cucumbers, and beans. The seeds of the latter came from the coast from gardener to gardener until they reached the interior where time gave them a local name and incorporated them into the tribal feasts.

The missionary distributed seeds such as tomatoes, cabbage, corn, and carrots, improved banana suckers, pineapples and papaw, as well as introducing citrus trees.

Pigs, an important factor in Dani economy, were used for currency and sacrifice. Boars were brought in to better the strain. The people were encouraged to keep poultry instead of dogs. With government aid, cattle were introduced, and backyard fishponds were built and furnished with fingerlings from coastal hatcheries.

Twice a week successful gardeners harvested their produce to sell at the station. Excess was "back loaded" on the plane to the coast. The people milled about thrusting their wares into the missionaries' faces, demanding that they buy. Rejected, inferior produce was persistently urged upon the buyers with loud shouts, "Buy this—buy mine."

"Bring half-ripe tomatoes, not these bruised overripe ones. Then we shall buy them," explained the missionary's wife.

Infuriated, the tomato seller hurled the red, squashy mass hard against her unsuspecting back.

Cunningly, the Danis packed bundles of beans so that the coarse were covered by the succulent. With the help of an accomplice, they tried to sell their wares twice over—and sometimes succeeded. A Dani assistant, set to shelling corn for the chickens would often slip cobs through the fence into a friend's waiting hand for him to resell.

When some law and order was injected into the trading, the missionaries took advantage of the crowds to tell them the real purpose of their coming and to help them find their third need, eternal life. A missionary settled the people down with some degree of quietness and reassured the persistent women who sidled up whispering, "I've got potatoes with golden skins. You buy them, don't buy the other women's—theirs are no good."

Then he took up a stone ax, asking, "Who made this ax?"

"Oh, that's Bokowarek's ax. He made it."

"Who made the stone?"

The Danis looked at each other questioningly.

Carrying Sweet Potatoes. Sweet potatoes brought to the missionaries were backloaded on the planes to the coast for sale there.

Then turning back to the speaker, "Well, who did make it? We don't know—you tell us."

Then the missionary taught them of God the creator.

Day after day they repeated the lesson until they could chant it to their own tunes, after the cultural pattern of their singing. One took the lead: "Who made the sun?" The chorus came in with the answer: "God made the sun."

One morning as the crowd sat on its haunches in a forest of spears and arrows, a small group sat off to the side taking no interest in the lesson.

A burly fellow from the listening group stood up, marched over to the outsiders, stamped a big black foot, and harangued them for not joining in. Back he went to the flannelgraph board, with the offenders meekly following. Turning to the board, he saw that the pictures had been removed.

"Who stole the sea, the stars, and the moon?" he bawled.

Receiving them from the missionary, he slammed them back into place. Then, with eyes blazing, he poured out the story to the now attentive delinquents.

From God's act of creation, the teachers went on to tell them of the fall of man.

"You mean to say that we all have one father, this man Adam? That the black man and the white man have a common origin?"

They liked the idea and wanted to know more of it.

"This man doesn't know about Adam. You tell him," said Kwamok, indicating his companion whom he had brought to Charles Horne.

Sitting down with him, Horne started the story.

"No. No. You haven't sung yet."

"That's really not necessary to the story," Charles told him.

In the Dani way of life, so much was religious ritualism— the direction of the slats in the house, the shape of the door, what they wore and how they put it on, what they ate and how they cooked it—that in their minds the missionaries' actions too became significant rites to be faithfully observed that merit may follow.

"Oh, I know," said one fellow, pondering the truths presented to them, "The white man walks with God, but we Danis, we've walked away from God."

Then the missionaries told them that sin too had a common origin. No man can keep the laws of God. No man can make his own way back to God by his own righteousness. God sent his Son, Jesus Christ, to be the way for all men, no matter who they are, to come to God.

Little by little the great doctrines were simply outlined so that, when the time came, the Danis would have a solid foundation on which to build faith in Jesus Christ.

Sometimes the talks were illustrated on the blackboard. The teachers drew some strokes and it looked like a tree. They drew some more strokes and there was a house. They drew other strokes and it didn't look anything at all, yet they said, "This says 'so and so.'" They made these same strokes on a piece of paper, gave it to a boy who took it to another missionary. The recipient looked at it and gave the boy a knife, an ax, or something to take back to the man who made the marks. Here was powerful magic!

When the missionary told the Danis that they would build a school to teach them how to make and understand the marks their enthusiasm abounded. They too would know this magic. But the teachers looked beyond to the time when the Danis would read the Word of God for themselves.

"Will we be like the white man then?" they asked. "Will we cut off our beards and hair and go to the big town and see God?"

And the missionaries asked themselves, "Will they ever realize that the kingdom of God is within them?"

When the school was built, the men, fully armed and feathered, massed together and raced in a body shouting and yelling around the building.

A little apprehensively the missionary inquired, "Why did you do that?"

"Oh, we were driving out the evil spirits. If our young people are going to have school, we must have it properly."

The first pupils, adolescent youths, were no school boys "with shining morning faces creeping like a snail unwillingly to school." They burst into the building, bounding from place to place to find a position to suit themselves. Onlookers, too, crowded in or hung through the windows obstructing light and air. The rancidity of pig fat and sweat offended the teachers' nostrils. Rows of flashing teeth grinned from soot-blackened, enthusiastic faces framed in long greasy ringlets.

Diffidently, the teachers suggested, "Don't you think you could wash a bit of this off before coming to school?"

"Oh, no," they protested, "The girls wouldn't look at us then."

Tapping feet and wriggling bodies, loud conversations, and rude interruptions indicated that not one pupil had ever been taught to listen while another talked. Available personnel for teaching were mainly women; and young Dani men had not learned to give respect to women. Obscene asides, sly titters, and outright refusals to cooperate did not help classroom discipline. One missionary's wife, trying to inject some discipline, spoke firmly to one of the lads. No woman was going to talk down to him. He fitted an arrow against his bow string and quivering with rage, threatened her with it. As she stood her ground, her faithful dog put the boy outside.

When the marks on the paper were not mastered in three easy lessons concentration flagged, interest waned, and attendance became spasmodic. They welcomed any diversion. Also, through the need of protection against a constant enemy, the youths came fully armed and placed their weapons around the schoolroom walls. A cry from the hills, and the school emptied as the entire class took up their arms and clambered through windows and doorways to join the pig hunt or threatened war. The teachers with a wry smile for the ways of those who live only for the present packed up their books to wait until the mood for learning brought their pupils back again.

A show of progress in making letters and spelling out the sounds encouraged the jaded teachers to continue. They knew that in the end some would win through.

8

Among Thieves

ON ARRIVAL at Bokondini the missionaries had been treated by the Danis with awed respect and even fear. When the people saw, however, that the white men were vulnerable humans and not impregnable spirits, they boldly helped themselves to the missionaries' goods and insolently challenged their superiority. Increased stealing added strain to the workers; anything put down unguarded was filched away. The wind sock was taken one night and probably cut up, rubbed until unrecognizable with soot and pig fat, and used for head caps. Work tools given out were not always returned. Each evening the work supervisor took careful tally and listened to some outlandish tales of the fate of the missing article.

"All right, no pay and no work for anybody until the shovel is returned," he would announce.

Group pressure usually brought back the missing object, although sometimes the employers had to hold out for a week or so.

One day sixty men were sent to cut fence posts. Twenty sharp axes were an unprecedented opportunity to cut timber for themselves as well as collecting a day's pay. Most of those posts cut that day were carried into the villages. The missionaries flogged their patience and strained their ingenuity to the limits to keep apace of the cunning devices of the Danis to outwit them.

Although they stole from the missionaries, the Danis knew that the Tuans, whom they respected as men of their word, would not steal from them. Often his home was a strong room for articles placed in safe deposit.

78

"Tuan, I've worked all these days," Kaniaganak said, showing his closed fists to Charles Horne. "I've received this ax as wages. Now can I keep it in your house?"

"Why do you want to keep it there?"

"If I take it to my house, it will be stolen, but you will keep it safely for me."

At the time when thieving was at its worst, the UFM commenced work in the Wolo Valley through which Bond, Dawson, and Veldhuis had passed three years before.

The missionary did not see the Dani as just a thief and a marauder, but as a man created by God. He saw him against the background of God's eternal intention for him. Knowing that the Dani had an integral part in the fulfillment of that purpose, the missionary entered the forbidding valley with the sure objective of restoring the lost Stone Age man to his full status in Christ. Aware that the Wolo Danis could be openly hostile, he went forward confident of the presence of invisible battalions.

The Wolo Valley was one range away, only a short day's walk from Pass Valley where the American Air Force C-47 had crashed in 1945. Metal arrow tips and homemade knives, tucked into Dani belts, indicated that they had made themselves practical souvenirs from the wreck of the "mother of steel." They had hidden the parachutes and other movable parts of the shattered aircraft in caves in the mountains, the traditional habitat of their ancestors' spirits. Whatever the thoughts were, locked in their superstitious minds, they boded no good for the white man.

The three men appointed to open the Wolo station, all rearing to go, were Bert Power, Garnet Ericson, and Wal Turner, called *Tuan Buluk* (the little Tuan) by the Danis. His small, wiry frame belied the Danis' conception that all white men were six-footers, like the other missionaries who had come to live among them.

Wal and his wife, Nan from Campsie in New South Wales, had spent two years helping the Baptists build their Baiyer Valley station in the Papuan highlands before coming to work with the UFM in West New Guinea. They had been living at Bokondini only a few months before Wal left for Wolo.

Heavy weather prevented the three Europeans and five Sengge men from leaving Bokondini for Wolo on the day scheduled. The clear early morning of Wednesday, March 15, 1957, was an answer to a pilot's prayer. The MAF pilot was to take the party to the Pyramid Rock where C&MA had built an airstrip and mission station. From there they would walk into the Wolo Valley to the airstrip site, selected on an air survey.

As they flew out of Bokondini, the Kelila side of the range was ablaze with burning houses set alight by the raiding Bokondinis. Those in the aircraft looked down with hearts stirred by the desperate need of men goaded to killing each other.

By eight o'clock, the pilot had made three shuttles and brought the men and their equipment to Pyramid. The Pyramid Danis were influenced from the Grand Valley and spoke the Baliem dialect, which was considerably different from the Western Dani spoken by the Bokondinis. The locals were restless, touchy, and habitual thieves. In between flights, the men had stayed on the airstrip, watching their gear. When the last load was in, they carried it the two hundred yards to the house to keep it under surveillance while they drank coffee with two Americans from the C&MA, who did all they could to help the three Australians open this new territory.

Although several mission societies sponsored and financed by different groups were now working in the many Dani valleys, each missionary helped the other to commence and maintain his work. They worked unitedly towards a common goal of establishing the church of God in this land.

When the survey patrol had walked through the Wolo Valley, the Pyramid and Wolo Danis had been one people. Sometime later a split had arisen and they became bitter enemies. Each blamed the other for the supreme insult of mutilating the other's dead in battle. Each gory fight resulted in new grizzly retaliatory defacements of enemy bodies.

A no-man's-land, as wide as an hour's walk, separated the two groups. A bunch of wily locals volunteered to show the party the track down to the river an hour away. It was soon evident that they were deliberately trying to mislead them. Four times they had to compel their unscrupulous guides to turn back and take them on the right path.

Heavy night rains on the watershed had brought flood waters whirling and eddying about the river. The fellows hitched up their clothes and waded out to the main course. By now many spear-waving Danis had gathered. Their wild talk and manner discomforted the party, who had difficulty in persuading some to pole them across the river on their rafts—three or four saplings tied together with cane. As they loaded the craft, the Australians' mistrust increased—there was more log under the water than above it.

When the fleet of rafts pushed into the river, Turner's crew separated from the rest and poled two or three hundred yards downstream to a side eddy. Although he knew only a few words of their language, he clearly understood their intent to do him mischief. Hiding his anxiety, he bluffed them into returning to the rest of the party.

Two hours later and some two hundred yards downstream from their starting point, the polesmen beached their raft. The trekkers paid the boatmen with cowrie shells, picked up their loads, and headed down the track. The Danis boldly pushed and harried them, leering in their faces and pulling at their clothes and packs. One tried to filch a knife from the sheath on Bert Power's hip. Others tried to get away with a bush knife given to them to cut saplings to carry the radio.

The party, disquieted by the crowding of the agitated Danis, hurried into no-man's-land where the Baliems halted and screamed after them. Alone and relieved, they took a faint trail which was apparently used by scouts through long grass. Kunai grass often marked a boundary, and when a crisis developed, the area was burnt off to be used as a battlefield.

They crossed and recrossed the winding Wolo river and numerous lesser streams by log bridges made slippery by many feet muddied in the slimy approaches. While crossing one of these greasy poles, Garnet Ericson's feet skidded to either side and he sat down with a hard and painful wallop.

As they entered a narrow gorge two or three hours inside the Wolo Valley a sentry high on a cliff face saw them and shrilled a warning. Heads popped up over the ridge to peer down at them. They waved and kept moving forward, aware that should the fellows on top turn hostile, they were trapped.

Well into the afternoon, Power said, scanning the hills, "I wonde·· where the people are? It's strange that we've seen so few."

"Yes, hope it doesn't mean that they are up to something. Those fellows on the hill know we are about. Something must be holding their attention," agreed Ericson.

"Listen, what's that?"

"Shouts of men returning from battle! So that's what has been keeping them," said Turner.

Red-eyed, sweating warriors, with upturned nasal pig tusks and nodding plumes trotted towards them, confirming their speculation.

"We're looking for flat ground on which the airplane can land," they explained in reply to the Papuans' questions.

The area which they had previously selected from an air survey and at which they had now arrived was too short. Power looked at his watch, "There's no time to look any further today. We'd better make camp here and radio the pilot not to come, or he'll be in at five o'clock as we arranged. We don't want building equipment dropped on this site."

"Hope we'll be able to get through," said Ericson. "The lad gave the transmitter a pretty sharp tap when he slipped on that river log."

They rigged the radio, hung the antenna, and tuned the dial, calling Bokondini.

Bokondini came in. "Bokondini to UFM mobile. Reading you—go ahead, please."

Power answered, "We've arrived at the site. It's too short.

Don't come over today. Come tomorrow after we have moved to a better place."

The knock on the river crossing had damaged the set and their transmission blurred out after the first sentence—"We've arrived at the site."

The pilot's eyes questioned the Bokondini missionaries clustered around the radio waiting to hear the party's progress.

"Well, they are there," he said, "Perhaps I should hop over. Maybe they are wanting the stuff or maybe they need help."

The Wolo campers heard the drone of the plane and groaned, "He didn't hear us."

Quickly they laid out a "don't drop" message on the grass. But it was not clear enough and confused the pilot into thinking that the drop was required. He circled again and flew in low as shovels, axes, and picks for building the air strip were thrown over. The men collected everything they could find and pitched it into a nearby garden hut, where the Danis cooked and slept while gardening.

More warriors returning home peered in at them. They were excited and tense, jumping up and jerking at their weapons at any movement from the white man. Ericson reached for matches and pulled one across the box filling the dark hut with a sudden flare of light. Frightening screams broke from the Danis as they pushed through the doorway. The more courageous peeped in again and whistled against the bent knuckle to find the flame imprisoned in the glass cage of a hurricane lantern.

Except for movements to and from the battleground, they saw nothing of the warriors the next day. Garnet Ericson and three Sengge boys returned to Pyramid to get another radio while the others searched for a more suitable site. They chose the same one where the survey patrol had camped when the Wolos had conferred together to murder them.

On Saturday, the war over, the Wolos flocked around the camp. With their usual noisy exuberance they helped carry the equipment over to the new site. Some were given axes and machetes to cut tent poles and to make a bush shelter.

Halfway through the morning, Power lifted his head to listen. "Those fellows should be coming back with some timber by now. Say! It's too quiet. Something's wrong. Hey! Where are all those Wolo boys?" he shouted.

"There's not one about," Simon, a Sengge man, called back. "Everyone's gone. They've taken the axes and knives and all the stuff they were carrying."

It took them several days, visiting village after village, listening to the same story of the thieves being over in the next village before they recovered all their goods.

The land, purchased from the Wolos for the strip, was an old garden site interlaced with deep drains. While the mission party were filling these with stones, the chief, Titlok, chewing on his lips to contain the anger boiling within him, came over to the missionaries and ordered them to stop the work and go home.

"If we go back to Bokondini, you'll not get medicine for all those yaws and ulcers that we are treating every day," they warned. Titlok thought that over and agreed to let them stay after he had extracted a promise that they would not fell the sacred pines at the end of the strip.

"We'll leave them," the missionaries agreed, "But it would be much easier for the pilot without them as they stand in the way of his approach."

Titlok sprinkled pig's blood near the trees and resigned himself to the presence of the missionaries, but not without pressure to get all he could from them. Never sure whether they would be forced out or left alive to finish their work, the men tried to humor the Wolos while keeping a rigid standard as a foundation for the future.

The Danis tried them sorely. As Simon left the strip one morning to go up to the house to get a marking line, a Wolo workman flung dirty words and yellow clay at him. Simon's patience broke. Picking up a stone he turned and hurled it at his insulter. The Wolo ducked and the stone flew over his head, missing him by a breath.

The three missionaries ran in alarm towards the boy. "Don't

ever do that again!" they admonished. "We've told you often if you want to live, you must hold your anger. That rock could have killed him."

Another day while a Dani was digging out a bank, the ground caved in and buried him. His people screamed in a frenzy, while the white men dug out his head and pulled him free. He was alive but shocked. The missionaries knew that they would pay the full price of a life for a life in the event of a fatal accident.

When the Australians built a bush hut and put a fence around it, after the manner of the Dani villages, the Papuans respected them more, and stealing dropped off, although every once in a while an ax or a knife disappeared.

After a month, Garnet Ericson and the Sengge boys walked out to Pyramid to bring in the MAF pilot so he could check the strip before making the first landing. On their return trip, the Wolo enemies in the Baliem turned hostile.

Ericson and the Sengge were now familiar with the track, but the Danis, running around them, tried to head them off into false paths. When they were caught wading through a water soak, the Papuans pelted them with stones and belittling insults. The Danis huddled in groups to confer and then, with their spears threatening, chased after the foreigners. Not knowing what was brewing in the primitive minds, Ericson and the pilot hurried towards the border.

"It's much easier to fly over these people than to walk through them," said the pilot with a Baliem spear prodding his ribs.

On the day of the first landing, Wal Turner went to the coast to be with his wife, Nan, for the birth of their first child. Ericson and Power continued finishing the strip and building the station.

Although not openly hostile, the people remained insolent, laughing at the message which the missionaries had brought. Odd skirmishes, threats of war, and battle talk kept them occupied. When the talk increased, the missionaries knew that something big was in the making.

One day nobody came to the mission. The valley, quiet with
an unwanted silence, seemed to have emptied of all human life,
save the two fellows building a better way for a people who
did not want it. Only the muted sound of wind and river, im-
pervious to the ways of man, mingled with the thud of hammer
blows.

Into the rural solitude of late afternoon broke the agitated
movement of fleeing women. Laden with string bags, some
crammed with their belongings, and others with small babies
and piglets stuffed in together; with children and pigs on a
leash running beside them, they streamed out of the top
valley and down along the airstrip.

Garnet Ericson and Bert Power intercepted them, "What is
happening?" they asked.

Breathlessly the women told them, "The Baliems have come.
Many men have been wounded and four are already dead."

Smoke arose above the trees down by the Wolo River, confirming their words.

"The Baliem people have crossed the river and are burning
the houses," Power said, as he and Ericson turned and hurried

PALLBEARERS. Wolos carry in their dead after the battle
with the Baliem tribe.

to a rise a couple of hundred yards from the house, from where they could look down onto the river flats.

They sat on a rock watching the grass huts belch heavy yellow smoke and break into angry, leaping flames. A sinewy fellow in paint and feathers and leading several others similarly garbed, dashed up the hill.

"Are there any Wolos about?" he asked his eyes darting in search of them.

"Who are you?" Power and Ericson inquired.

"We are from Baliem."

"Well you go right back there. This is not your land. This belongs to the Wolos," they advised.

With intention to scare away this intruder's fellow warriors looting and burning in the houses below, Ericson fired his rifle into the air. The leader turned and went back down to them. Ericson and Power followed him, hoping to prevent further slaughter by persuading the Baliems to return home.

Some were inclined to take their advice and go, but one big fellow excited by the fury of burning houses, the loot of enemies, and the sense of mastery stood like a rock with his barrel chest thrust out, long pig tusks quivering in his nose and arrogance questioning in his eyes—"Who are you?"

The Wolos on the top of the hill had regathered their forces and crept down under cover of the bush. As they closed in, the hillside became alive with shrieking men. Three Baliem boys standing apart were cut down. At ten yards a Wolo shot arrows into a tormented Baliem face, tearing it to pieces.

Ericson and Power turned away, sickened to the pits of their stomachs. Twenty or so lay dead. They had wanted only to stop the butchery, not to take sides, but the Baliems swore to shoot them if ever they put foot in the Grand Valley.

"If only the Baliems had gone home when we told them," said Power, shaking his head over the pitiful waste of life.

"It's no use telling them not to fight or in trying to break it up. They are born to it. Only a changed heart can alter their attitude. We must concentrate on that. But it's pretty hard to sit by without intervening while they kill each other."

"True, but however many fights we might break up, we would never eradicate the motivating factor that way. They would just break out again and again. War is an integral part of their religion which only Christ can replace," said Power as he and Ericson conversed and prayed together that night in their thatched hut on the edge of the airstrip.

A month later a large Baliem party again invaded Wolo territory in an attempt to avenge their dead. The Wolos, pre-warned of their movements, ambushed and killed many, while losing only one of their own men.

The victors, tying the enemy dead by the feet, dragged them around in a public display of contempt, while frenzied onlookers kicked and spat at the mutilated bodies. They tore the necklaces, spirit fetishes, from the corpses and threw them into a heap. Titlok knelt on them, sat on them, and jumped on them intermittently screaming and running back and forth in a fanatical effort to get these enemy spirits onto the Wolo side.

Spears, arrows, bows, and a couple of bush knives—probable souvenirs from the drop to the Survey Patrol on the top of Mud Pass—taken from the dead were stacked near the sacred pine trees by the gloating conquerors. Leaves smeared with pig fat were waved over these weapons as the Wolos appealed to their ancestral spirits.

Allied groups assembled at different places close to the scene of the battle. Standing opposite to each other, about a hundred yards apart, they held the captured spears aloft while calling again on the spirits. Then one group ran whooping to another group where the weapons were again held high and the spirits invoked. This continued until the ceremony was completed. Then they built a special house for these weapons which became war fetishes.

The Wolos burned some of the dead so that the smoke rising from the funeral pyre might stimulate the sorrow of their enemy in the valley beyond. With malevolent delight they threw some into the river to float past the Baliem villages. Others they left for the pigs to eat. Months, and even years later, the bones still lay scattered about, a symbol of their victory. They had crowned their triumph with vicious insult, establishing themselves as lords of the valley.

The victory increased the tension among the Wolos. They reinforced their lookout scouts on the hills. Every morning a band marched to the river to watch for retaliatory raiders from the Baliem.

The Wolos did not sing at their work as the Bokondinis had. When Bert Power started the motor to charge the radio batteries, Titlok approached him. "Please don't let that thing talk. We want to hear the warning cry should the enemy come."

The missionaries stopped the engine and ran it at night.

Sneak forays continued, killing the unguarded ones and twos. The wariness and tension sharpened Wolo tempers. The sense of victory increased their arrogance.

Mission personnel changed at Wolo. Ross Bartel, back from linguistic school, replaced Bert Power, who had gone south to Australia on furlough. Wal Turner had returned to Wolo from the coast, and Garnet Ericson had moved over to Katupaka to help the Regions Beyond Missionary Union commence their work in the Swart Valley, west of Bokondini.

The men had built a small dispensary where each morning they tended the medical cases, which included many battle wounds. A big fellow from the Ilugwa pushed in one morning demanding a "needle." When this treatment, an injection from the hypodermic needle, was refused as not being suitable for his ailment, he became defiant.

Bartel firmly put him outside to wait and simmer down. But his anger boiled. He came back and thrust a spear close to the throat of Bartel's open-necked shirt. With a show of indifference to the quivering spear and the blazing-eyed Ilugwa, Bartel continued with his treatments for fifteen minutes, before the locals, satisfied with his mettle, pulled the incensed fellow off and sent him about his business.

Nan Turner and baby Bruce had hoped to follow Wal into Wolo a few days after his return. When Asian flu broke out on the coast, killing scores of coastal Papuans, rigid quarantine prevented all movement to the highlands. Mrs. Turner and the baby were kept six weary weeks at Sentani. On Saturday, the last day in August, the restrictions lifted, and she flew into Wolo where she was almost smothered by the curious and excited Danis crowding to see this white woman and her baby.

On the previous day, another machete had been stolen. Because the restive Danis were growing increasingly bolder, and thieving was becoming more brazen, the Wolo missionaries had tightened their attitudes towards stealing in an attempt to hit it hard. The Wolo's victory against the Baliem had inflated their sense of mastery. Two lone men with a "wealth" of goods were a constant challenge to them, and only the invisible forces of God stayed their hands from wiping them out.

Across the valley, the Danis harrassed the Pyramid missionary families. They took clothes from their lines, taunting the owners, "When you give us shells, we shall return them to you."

Coupled with the Dani overbearing offensiveness, the unceasing stealing had grown to be almost insufferable.

The next morning, Wal Turner and Ross Bartel went to retrieve the stolen knife. On finding the first three villages empty, the two men separated. The Danis, who were expecting the Australians, had hidden in the bush. Now, they came running out, crouching low with bow string taut and arrows aimed at Bartel. He called them to stop. Unheeding, they kept advancing. Bartel fired a shot over their heads. The leader shot his arrows in quick succession. Bartel dodged and fired at the warrior's feet. The Dani stalled a moment and then came on, shooting rapidly.

Bartel knew then that a gun fired to scare was useless once the attackers had pulled his bluff. A rifle in his hands and a Dani roused to kill at thirty paces—Bartel's finger touched the trigger—he could not miss. But he had not come to kill the Danis. He relaxed his finger, whipped about, and breaking from them, ran through the bushes.

Turner heard the shots and ran towards Bartel. Coming out at the top of the village he called, "Don't back out! Stop and talk to them." "I've already tried that!" yelled Bartel.

The Danis closed in on Turner. Seeing that they meant to

fight he put down his gun and holding out his hand went towards them. "We're your friends," he said, "We're not your enemies. We don't want to fight you."

Spurning his friendly gesture, Peledek, the leader, released his drawn bowstring, shooting Turner in the chest. Wal pulled the arrow, but only the shaft and a gush of blood came away, leaving the six-inch bamboo tip inside. Another Dani, with anger leaping in his eyes, came at him with poised spear. Standing unarmed in their midst, Turner looked at him with an unusual calm. The fellow fell back and lowered his spear.

This hesitancy gave both Turner and Bartel time to get along the homeward track. The Danis rallied and came after them.

Pain, weakness, and chest congestion slowed Turner's pace. Bartel hurried ahead to high ground above the river to locate the Danis whom they seemed to have shaken off. But, they had come by another route and were closing in on the house to cut off the return of the two men. Fearing for Nan Turner alone with the baby, Bartel left Turner and ran down to the station to outrace the Papuans. A shower of arrows hailed around him as he dashed into the yard.

Nan Turner had been so absorbed in preparing a meal to celebrate the coming of a woman to the man's camp, that she had given little attention to the outside activities. When Bartel came bounding into the house calling, "Put Bruce away from the windows and keep under cover—the Danis have turned against us," she was startled into an awareness of the dangerous mob outside.

Bartel called for help on the radio. He called the mission at base, air radio at Sentani and Biak, called anybody who might hear, but no one responded. The Danis, yelling and threatening, came up to the fence. One tried to break through with an arrow aimed at the window. Bartel warned him and he retreated. Further up the strip the Danis had broken into Turner's partly built house and were spilling over each other to grab loot for themselves.

Bartel thought grimly, *In their minds they have already won this showdown.*

Nan Turner had taken up a flare pistol, and watching beside the window of the room where her baby slept, listened for her husband's return. She crept to the front of the house and peeped through the window. She saw him then, crouching screened from the Danis, in a deep drain on the other side of the airstrip.

Turner had pushed himself this far. Through senses blurred by pain and faintness, he saw the steep bank before him and knew that somehow he must crawl over it and down the airstrip past the crazed mob, to get into the house to reach his wife and infant son.

While he rallied his strength, a group of Danis led by Titlok came down from the mountain to stand by the missionaries. They challenged the attackers, thus distracting their attention and allowing Turner to get to the house. At the gate he turned and looked into a hate-distorted face behind a bowstring tightened on an arrow. It was the man who had shot him. He ducked behind the paling fence, staggered to the shelter of the door, which Nan had opened to receive him, before the fellow could get into position again.

Although shocked, Turner was controlled by an inner calm that comes only from the deep resources of God. With trained fingers Nan tightly bound the wound. She found morphine and injected it along with a heavy dose of penicillin to work against the filth that went into his body on the arrow tip. Escaping air from his lung constricted his throat and swallowing sustaining fluids became increasingly difficult. The rust-colored blood confirmed that the lung had been punctured, but whether the heart was damaged or other serious trouble caused, Nan had no way of telling. The uncertainty gnawed at her through the long afternoon as she watched her husband's grey face and failing strength.

Her prayer was a desperate cry, "Oh Lord, let them hear us. Let them hear and send a plane." But the radio was dead. The hum of a listening station tuned in, raised their hopes, but no one responded. Air Radio Medang came in, calling its aircraft. Hope sprang up in their hearts as they called again. But despondency crushed that hope when Madang ceased transmitting.

"We're just not strong enough to reach them," despaired Bartel, letting his head fall into his hands.

Nan's special dinner dried in the pans. She stirred the fire and made a cup of tea.

Although Titlok's group had driven the attackers back, there was the possibility of them increasing their force through confederation with another group.

The missionaries' hopes centered on the C&MA four o'clock radio check with its inland stations. Although the UFM operated on a different frequency, it was close enough for the possibility of their call being heard.

One by one the C&MA stations gave their traffic and went off the air.

"Mission Sentani to Tulim."

The last call. Bartel shouted into the microphone only to hear in reply, "Good afternoon, Tulim out."

The finality tore at their hearts. Then Tulim was coming in again.

"Station calling Tulim; say again, please."

"Thank you God!" breathed Nan, "They've heard."

C&MA Sentani had heard enough to know that Wolo was under attack. They alerted Charles Horne who was in Sentani at that time. He called the MAF pilot. Within ten minutes the plane was flying into the highlands, snaking its way through towering clouds filled with lightning and rain. The missionaries on the hill at Sentani stood by the radio, following his flight, visualizing every cloud-obscured mountain menacing his safety, praying against probable attack to his aircraft on landing. The pilot's wife sat with them, screwing the hem of her skirt into a tight twist, the only outward sign of her personal anxiety. Her friends saw and noted the courage of this woman who could see her husband go into danger to help others.

The pilot flew first to Hettigima and picked up a doctor, then landed safely at Wolo. The doctor, on seeing Turner, said, "Let's get him out of here where I can give him better attention."

After taking the Turner family back to Hettigima and flying to Wamena to get a government officer and two policemen, the daylight had gone. As they turned into Wolo again, a curtain of rain and darkness hung across the valley. Through the murkiness the pilot picked out the strip tucked between the mountains.

With a pressure lamp at the top end of the strip and Ross Bartel with a flashlight at the bottom end, the pilot began circling. In an endeavor to keep away from the mountains, his first and second passes were too high. Satisfied with the third pass he came in; as he touched the ground, his lights showed only empty space. He applied his brake hard and stopped the Cessna from pitching into the drop beyond.

With the coming of the airplane and nightfall, the Danis had returned to their villages. Turner's assailant had looked up, seen the blazing landing lights, and had rushed out into the darkness, assured that these were the eyes of God searching for him.

Next day Wal Turner was taken to a hospital. The arrow had narrowly missed the heart, puncturing the lung. He still carries the tip and a renewed sense of trust in God and responsibility to his fellowmen. The same day, two chiefs persuaded the people to return everything looted from the vacant house, as well as the stolen machete. They obeyed, even to bringing three pigs as a peace offering.

At this time, away in South Australia, Ross Bartel's home state, a woman asked her friend, "Do you know if there is a missionary called Bartel working anywhere?"

The friend thought for a moment, "Oh, yes, there's a Ross Bartel up in West New Guinea."

"I've never heard of him before. Yet on the third of September I felt strangely compelled to pray for a missionary with the name of Bartel."

9

A New Village for Christ

THE MISSION HOME COUNCIL, ever ready to protect its mission-aries, questioned the advisability of Mrs. Turner returning to Wolo. Charles Horne wrote to the Melbourne office, "I do not question the rightness of sending a woman to Wolo, particu-larly when that woman is Nan Turner. She would be a greater asset under dangerous circumstances than some men. I do not hesitate to allow their return since both Wal and his wife are keen to go."

Back at Wolo, Turner's first heart-constraining obligation was to make friends with his assailant. Peledek extended a dubi-ous hand. *Was this some treachery? No wounded man sought out his enemy but to retaliate.* When Turners chose Peledek's son to be their house boy, and when Peledek himself was wounded and Mrs. Turner saved his life by removing the arrowhead, he knew that they loved him with a strange love beyond his understanding.

The Dani is no slower than any other to discern sincerity. The missionary soon learns that the language of love is a major entry into any people. Nevertheless, unless a missionary learns the natural language of the people, he is only an audience watching a mime. A saga of life and death passes before him. He remains outside, scarcely piecing the story together, until he understands their language. Then he becomes a vital actor in the pageant itself.

Wal Turner had no intention of staying on the outside. After doing a course with the Summer Institute of Linguistics, he la-conically stated, "It has taught me one thing, which is that I'll never be a linguist."

He was essentially a practical man with trained natural ability in mechanical skills. While at the coast recuperating from his wound, he explored the war junk heaps and found old bomber superchargers, which he put to turning water into electricity. This saved the mission hundreds of dollars in both lighting and power fuel and its air freight inland.

At Wolo, however, Turner faced up to the issue that if he did not give the gospel to these people in their own tongue, they would never hear it. With the help of Myron Bromley's linguistic material on this dialect, he set himself to master the language. He became a fluent speaker, conversing privately and spending himself in his preaching, as well as making worthwhile contributions at missionary linguistic conferences. When commended on his linguistic achievements, he said, "Nobody knows what it cost me." He paid the price with his health.

The Wolo warlords recognized the gospel preaching as a challenge to their authority. They saw that whoever accepted it must give their allegiance to God and practice what it taught. They knew too that this would leave them without a following. Therefore, they opposed the teaching and made open ridicule of the twice weekly meetings. Paternal group leaders forbade their villagers to attend. Some ignored the threats and not only listened to the messages but learned them.

The women missionaries, Nan Turner, Lil Bond, and Marjory Arthur (later Heyblom), now stationed at Wolo, commenced knitting classes to attract the women and, at the same time to enable them to hear and memorize the Scripture. Irate husbands stopped their wives saying, "You have no time for knitting, you should be out in the gardens and minding the pigs."

When the missionaries brought out colorful wool for the women to knit caps for husbands, the men relented.

"Oh well," they conceded, "Go along and learn to knit me a cap, but don't listen to their words."

Operating maternal and baby welfare clinics, setting broken bones, and curing many ills, as well as sharpening their new steel axes, teaching school, introducing a better strain of breeding boar for their sows, and many other small services won their confidences, yet all this still did not break through the opposition of influential leaders—except one, Tamane. He was the young war leader who, when the missionaries first passed through his village on their way to Lake Archbold from Hettigima, had sensed that their coming was a good omen.

Although not yet thirty years old, Tamane could account for more than twenty men slain on the battlefield. Tribesmen spoke his name with respect and the enemy marked him for a prize. Already he was a man with two wives, Engali and Minakai.

He had befriended the Sengge boys who had stayed seven months at Wolo. They tried to tell him about God and the reason for the presence of the white man.

"Later," they said, "the missionaries will tell you about Jesus."

With his hands clenched around the shaft of a spear driven into the ground, Tamane would sit listening to Turner's preaching. *Is this what the Sengges were talking about?* he asked himself. *Is this what they were trying to tell me?*

One day Wal Turner squatted with Tamane by his family fire. Minakai took a potato from the coals and passed it to him. He broke it open and ate with them.

"We missionaries have not always known God," he said, "There was a time when I did not know Him. Then I began to hear God speaking to me and I listened to His words and obeyed them."

Tamane rubbed a thumb knuckle against his thin, finely shaped nose, nodded, and looked at Turner with honest eyes.

"Years ago I knew that God was trying to make Himself known to me," he answered, "Bond, Dawson, and Veldhuis came through this valley. They camped right here, where the mission houses are! Something inside me told me these were good men, that they were messengers of God. I wanted to be friends with them.

" 'I will sell them a pig,' I said to the other Wolo men.

" 'No, no,' they answered. 'The spirits are in them. If you do, your stomach will swell.'

"I did not listen to their words. I heard the voice inside
and sold them a pig. And you know, Tuan, my stomach did not
swell."

He paused and looked intently at Turner.

"Ever since then, I have been eating forbidden food to test
the old men's words—but nothing they predicted has happened."

He ate his potato in silence before continuing.

"When you came back, my heart was glad, because I knew
God was coming with you. The old men have told us what
their fathers told them. All these years we have been deceived. Now I know God. He tells me true."

While Tamane thirsted after truth revealed in Jesus Christ,
the other Wolo leaders kept aloof, jealously guarding their authority. Meanwhile, outside this valley a movement towards
the gospel by fetish burning was sweeping through the western districts.

Tamane wished to join this movement, but he was bound by
his group. Although fetishes were individually owned, they
were not the exclusive property of the owner, but functioned
within the group for the protection of the whole tribe. For
Tamane to live as an individual and burn his fetishes would not
only antagonize the group, but in their eyes would jeopardize
their battle security. Yet he knew that while he held his
fetishes he was tied to his old customs and group obligations.
While carrying out his responsibilities, his mind could not
receive the truth. He realized too that he could not perfunc-
torily carry out tribal rites, while intellectually pursuing
Christian teaching.

One day he surreptitiously burned some of his spirit symbols.
Because of the nature of these fetishes, the burning could not
be concealed for long.

The old men stormed against him, "Do you want to make us
vulnerable to our enemies?"

But Tamane would not comply with their demands.

When the villagers joined together to fence their neighbors'
gardens, they refused to help Tamane with his. They stole his

pigs instead. Sneers and abuse ostracized him from village fellowship. For twelve months after his conversion to Christ he remained in his village, but refused to worship or sacrifice to the spirits. Despite their animosity towards him, Tamane maintained a real concern for his people and helped them where he could.

Gradually the few who wanted the message looked upon him as a spiritual counselor. When their lives were threatened, he encouraged a younger convert, "Do not fear. If our people kill us, we shall go to our big Brother Jesus."

As his way of life became less compatible with that of his own village people, he built his own village on the other side of the airstrip. He explained to his wives, "This will be a Christian village. Here we shall talk about God and Jesus Christ. There will be no sorcery, no spirit worship, and no taboos. The village will be clean. There will be no pigs living in our house. We shall build them their own quarters."

He looked searchingly at each wife in turn, "If you come and live with me in that village, the people will treat you as they have me. You can choose if you will come with me or go back to your people."

"We will come with you," they answered.

"All right," he smiled, "Let's get started by asking God to help us."

Emelugun, a young unmarried man and a promising warrior who had accepted the teachings of Christ, joined Tamane in building the village. Although these two men were of different tribal groups, they joined together against the opposition of the war leaders, and a deep friendship developed. The unity of the believers in Christ had begun to break down tribal barriers.

At a later date, they publicly burned their fetishes, thus severing themselves from their groups. Emelugun, an intelligent man with keen spiritual perception, could make clear decisions on doubtful issues. Being a natural leader and speaker, he was given extra instruction so that he could teach those inquiring about the Christian way of life.

Emelugun's severance from the tribe jeopardized his chances of taking a wife. He wanted one who followed the Lord, not a girl who had been smeared with the purifying pig's blood and washed in the river to cleanse her of premarriage defilement. He knew that only the blood of Jesus Christ could remove the defilement of sin. He did not want his friends to collect pig's blood in wooden dishes, sprinkle it with salt dug from the hills and then, mopping it up with ferns, stuff it into their mouths to cajole the spirits into prospering the marriage. He had no heart to see his bride with the skin of the ceremonial pig draped over her head while the legs and hoofs dangled against her shoulder and thighs. He wanted his marriage to be as the Bible described; therefore, he would wait for a Christian wife.

Tamane broke with tribal convention when he built a house where, as head of the family, he could live with his wives. Here he could teach Christian living daily to his children and not just instruct them in the tradition of their fathers on special initiation days.

Enggali, Tamane's second wife, yearned for a child, but none came. Her family pressed her to sprinkle the blood of the sacred swine, but she refused, saying, "Those things are not Christian. If God wishes, He will give me a child."

Very soon after she took this position she conceived, confounding the elders and overcoming opposition. When the child was born, Tamane neither killed a spirit pig nor split the child's ear.

All Dani domestic pigs have the ear split. Tradition recalls a pig, with its ear unsplit becoming possessed with a demon and running into the bush. Now all wild pigs, whose ears, of course, no one had slit, are regarded as spirit-possessed. To guard against the same type of spirit possession, every newborn child has its ear lacerated.

Enggali took her baby to the welfare clinic and learned to give him vitamin-enriched tomatoes, a food tabooed to the tribe because of its association with the white man whose spirit origin was still unproved. The people watched and many tongues predicted a frightful end for the child. But Tamane had long learned that the eating of special foods had no power nor had the breaking of taboos any propensity for evil. When the little boy grew fatter and stronger than any other child, the villagers began to question the truth of their traditions. But most decided to wait and see, feeling sure that the spirits would have their revenge.

In a hill village, Menarek's wife had become ill with a severe infection. Rumors of her sickness filtered through to the mission.

"Bring her in so we can give her medicine," the missionaries pleaded.

"Oh no, we don't need your medicines. Her husband is a special medium for this kind of sickness. He is making very strong magic."

When, despite all his incantations and sacrifices she grew steadily worse, her people brought her to the missionaries. By then her condition was past the help of medicine.

Tamane told Menarek, "You trust God and ask Him. Only He can help your wife."

Tamane prayed for the man and woman who themselves had no faith, while the missionaries, trusting in God to do a miracle, nursed her and gave her what medication they could. It pleased God to restore her. The Christians' faith was encouraged, but the majority of Wolos remained hard and unbelieving.

Another time Tamane was again tested. Late one afternoon his wife Minakai and a friend hurried home from the gardens under a gathering storm. Lightning cut through the blackness of the clouds spilling out rain into the upper reaches of the river. The thunder rolled nearer. With necks thrust forward to balance the potato-filled bags heavy on their backs, the two women waded into the water.

Already the river had risen. The current rushed against their legs, swirled around their knees, and swept them off their feet. Villagers, hearing their screams, ran to help them.

They saw Minakai's friend struggling against the flood. A chain of hands pulled her exhausted onto the bank.

"Minakai, where's Minakai?" she panted.

Minakai was nowhere to be seen. Searchers ran up and down the stream scanning the turbulent waters; probing with poles its dark depths. They called her name, but the rush of water and tearing of the storm covered their voices.

Some of the men, Wal Turner among them, ran downstream. Scrambling out on the rocks they waited, hoping to grab Minakai's body as it swept past. But it did not come.

"The spirits have taken her away. This is their revenge against Tamane," the garrulous babbled.

Twenty minutes later, someone cried, "There she is!"

"Where?"

"Down there—wedged between those two boulders."

The men jumped into the icy water and pulled at the boulders to free her. Lifting her clear, they lay her down on the river bank. Then women began to wail.

Turner saw her chest move. "Look!" he said, "She's breathing. She's still alive but unconscious."

While he sent somebody to his house to get blankets and hot water bottles, he applied artificial respiration.

"There's practically no water in her lungs," he marveled. "There must have been an air vent down there between those two rocks."

Minakai remained unconscious for three hours. The Turners had taken her into their home, where she lived for several weeks, before she was sufficiently recovered to return to her family.

Bidi, an influential chief from the Ilugwa, came to the Turners. "Tuan," he said, "Now we know that you care for us. At first we weren't sure. We didn't know why you helped us. But because you took this woman into your home for many days, we know that you love us."

But even Bidi, accepting the missionaries' friendship, help, and love, could not yield his authority to One greater than he.

For a time he viciously turned against those whom he had acknowledged as true benefactors to his people.

"Can't you see," Tamane continued to plead, "that although the spirits are angry, they have no power against me while I believe in God? God, who does only good, is greater than the spirits who always bring evil upon us."

A Dani youth, Arikatdlek, was named the child of these spirits. Many a night the villagers stiffened, the skin contracting on their bodies.

"What is it?" the missionaries would ask.

"The spirits are in Arikatdlek again."

Under supernatural compulsion, the young man had rushed into the night trailing a thin, eerie wail. His cries grew louder until he was screaming with terrifying abandon. Men ran after him, tied him up, and with sorcery locked the spirits within his body, lest they should enter another. His people knew of no way to release Arikatdlek from their mastery, but only how to hold them down temporarily, leaving the man limp and spent.

But Christ has the authority to say, "Come out" and to destroy their power. One day Arikadtlek went to the missionary and said, "Tuan, I want Jesus to come into my heart."

They prayed together, Arikadtlek's act of faith consummating his salvation in Christ. When Christ came in, there was no place for the spirits. From that time on, he had no recurrence of these fits.

Yet the tribal leaders shut their eyes, preferring to be big men in bondage than to be free men in Christ. While accepting many of the benefits, they continued to oppose the sovereignty of the gospel.

Yet the caliber of the men like Tamane, Emelugun, and Arikadtlek assured the missionaries that believers who emerged from the opposition would form a solid church.

10

The Valley of Castoffs

DAVE COLE stared at the boots on his feet. The more he stared, the bigger they seemed to grow and the more they grew, the more the aching soreness inside them grew. To ease the ache he dropped down, draping his body over a flat rock. Eleven startled Dani carriers eyed his closed eyes and relaxed jaw, and they exclaimed, "Is he dead? Is Tuan dead true?"

Dave was too weary to move; he just fervently wished that he were "dead true." Better to lie forever on that trail and have his bones picked clean by vultures than to walk on blistered feet either back to Bokondini or over those endless ridges stretching three days to Mulia. At least, his fuzzy mind reasoned, he wouldn't have to walk to heaven in those boots. He didn't think that angels wore hiking boots; perhaps, he too, could get a pair of wings.

When the call to eat the evening meal came, as Dave half rolled and half flopped off the slab and propped his back against it, there was a moment of silence among the Danis as they tried to figure out this white man's trick of self-resurrection.

Dave Cole, a wiry Canadian trained at the Toronto Bible College, had married Dina Reimeyer, the WAC who had escaped the Baliem air crash. In July of 1958 they joined the Americans who had entered the West New Guinea program providing the personnel for the Mulia advance. Bryan University graduates Ralph and Melba Maynard, the first of the North American team, already had been at Bokondini twelve months, toughening up and getting acquainted with the Danis

104

as well as with Australian colloquialisms. They had been in West New Guinea only a few days when the central Baliem Danis attacked Wolo. Maynard, sent in to help, ran into trouble with the Australian language.

When he stooped to pat Wal Turner's big bedraggled dog, Bartel explained his emaciated condition, "The poor thing shot through when the fighting started."

Maynard ran his hands over the dog's lean body. "Where's the arrow hole?" he asked.

Bartel laughed. "I said 'shot through,' an Aussie colloquialism meaning 'ran away.' He ran away and so he has not been properly fed for a few days."

Maynard was not to live that down.

The Australians and Americans not only learned each other's idioms, but one complemented the other, as each contributed from his national background to the evangelism of a primitive people.

Bert Power cut his furlough short, postponed his marriage and returned to West New Guinea to lead the advance into Mulia due west of Bokondini on a tributary of the Upper Rouffaer River in August 1958. Leon Dillinger, who had come from Pennsylvania in May of that year, Ralph Maynard, and Dave Cole were the other team members. Despite trial climbs over the Bokondini ridges, Cole and Dillinger, fresh from city traffic, were unprepared for the hard, steep climbing. Power usually was fit for mountaineering, but now softened by furlough and struggling with new boots, he found the trek strenuous. At the end of the first day Dave Cole collapsed exhausted onto a flat rock. A night's rest and the next day's walk, however, saw progress in the hardening of their bodies to the arduous trekking which was to become a routine acitvity.

The Bokondini youths who were accompanying them, knowing they must pass through enemy hamlets, had stripped themselves of their clan identifications, cut their hair, and dressed in shorts and undershirts. They changed their names to Peter, James, and other Bible characters, and then, to their confusion, forgot who was who. They spoke in whispers so that their tongue would not betray them to their enemies. But they need not have feared, as their appearance was so changed that these Danis accepted them as "white" men. Although not previously sighted by Danis in this area, the white man was a much discussed topic. "White," regardless of the color of the skin, was applied to all who dressed and lived like the people who came from Hollandia. Thus, coastal Papuans were also called "white men."

The new settlers' reputation had become so favorable that all along the route the people begged them to stay. Only once were they challenged, when a frightened man barred their way with a drawn bow. Power, seeing the germ of reconsideration flick across the Dani's face, stepped quietly forward and gently took the arrow from the fellow's bow, and with a friendly hand on his shoulder reassured him.

That evening Ralph Maynard cooked fritters over the camp fire. "What's in the fritters?" someone asked. "*Dumas*," answered Maynard, naming a type of banana.

"*Dumas!*" ejaculated two Bokondini youths. "We've eaten *dumas?* They are taboo to us."

Two days later they said, "We've not died. We've not even been sick. Old Jukwanak lied to us."

"Well, don't go home and tell him so," cautioned Maynard. "He's the chief and you are only young boys. But, don't forget that the eating of *dumas* didn't have power to hurt you."

The boys began to suspect the untruth of the age-old superstitions.

As the patrol entered the Mulia valley, the people changed. Some watched their approach, vacantly staring from nonunderstanding eyes. Others talked to them, but the talk conveyed no intelligent communication. Little children, making animal noises and spasmodic, uncontrolled movements, sat in their mother's laps. Pendulous goiters stretched from ear to ear and hung on the chests of the mothers. The missionaries, horrified, felt they had stumbled into some repulsive dream world. The carriers, however, looked at each other knowingly and begged their leaders, "Go back, don't go any further. Anyone who comes here gets this sickness. The place is full of mad people."

"Ever since we first mentioned coming to Mulia, the Bokondinis have been telling us not to go to these crazy people who look like this," said Maynard, clenching two fists under his chin, "but their condition is more serious and widespread than I believed."

"They are a valley cast off by the rest of the Dani community," he added, giving the place the name the Valley of Castoffs.

The carriers were not wrong when they said that all who entered the valley caught the sickness, but this was not due to evil witchcraft as they believed. It seems that the Mulias came from the Baliem. Although recent migrants are generally bright, even some of them, as early as two years after their arrival, developed huge goiters and the resultant cretin symptoms.

That first night in the valley it rained hard. An old man sat in the ashes of a dying fire while the rain spilled over him. He flapped his hands and laughed, without even the basic sense to get in under shelter.

When the Mulias realized that the white man had chosen to live with them, their excitement leaped to a pitch. They would build a house! Everyone pranced about shouting orders which no one obeyed. The missionaries built their own shack. Whenever they were inside it, even from the first peep of dawn, the same imbecilic face grinned in at them, filling the one small window.

Every day the same handful of miserable half-deranged people came to stare at them, but made no response towards work.

"Hi, are there any more men in your village? Where are the others?" the missionaries asked.

Wide, vacant grins spread over the Dani faces.

"They are over at the Sinac, feasting."

"When are they coming back?"

The fellows grinned again, jigged a bit, hopped a little, and flapped their hands.

"Oh, tomorrow."

Every day the missionaries asked the same question and received the same answer until they despaired of receiving another.

Eventually, they managed to persuade some of these men to gather into heaps the thousands of stones scattered over the strip site. These people had not before sold their labor and had no understanding that they were to be paid for their work. At the end of the day the missionaries tried to form the uncomprehending workers into a line. Amid the confusion Dave Cole grabbed the leader, clamped a cowrie shell in his hand, and pushed him on his way. The fellow stood looking at the shell in his palm. He picked it up and examined it. A smile broke over his face. He had caught the idea and so had the rest. Line up, pass along, and get a shell. Soon the missionaries recognized the same faces passing along the line again and again!

Out came their little metal discs. They explained that in the morning each worker would get a disc and on presenting it in the evening he would get a shell for the work done. The Danis grinned and flipped their hands again. The incomprehensible white man—for picking up a few stones he would give a cowrie shell. Utopia had come to Mulia.

Ralph Maynard wrote to his mother:

"The people here! Oh, if you could see them! They are the most degraded, inhuman animallike nonanimals I have ever seen. Many of them are cretins, disfigured and deformed. More than half have goiters—some as large as footballs. But God loves them and wants to redeem them, so here we are."

Disappointment in their assignment, added to loneliness, intensified their physical weariness.

Tired of pumping the hand generator and making little impression on their failing radio batteries, the four men planned to have a gas driven generator flown to the C&MA station at Ilaga. Dave Cole, Leon Dillinger, and five Bokondini boys were to walk the three days through to Ilaga and pick it up.

On the first day out towards the Sinac, they met the long-

VALLEY OF CASTOFFS. More than half of the Danis in the Mulia Valley had oversized goiters.

expected warriors returning over the hill like a swarm of bees looking for a place to settle. Dillinger and Cole eyed them apprehensively, but they showed only surprise to see a white man in that place and continued on their way.

The Dillinger-Cole party followed a trade route, lost it in the undergrowth, and beat the bush searching for a way back to it.

"Not many Danis have travelled this way for years, I should say," commented Dillinger.

An indistinct trail and three days without seeing population showed that the Danis had chosen another route over which to trade their salt and green ax stones.

All one day, eleven hours, they climbed the ten thousand feet to the Ilaga Pass. One hour from the top, night caught them. Under an overhanging rock, zipped into sleeping bags, they huddled close to the fire. Not long from hustling activity of populated cities, isolated and unprotected in a night filled with whispering superstitious suggestions and the treachery of the untried, the two men measured their faith in God against the unknown.

Listening to the steady, irritating drop of moisture from the forest trees and rocks, Leon Dillinger wondered *Is the presence of God sufficient to sustain a man if lost?* Back in the States, surrounded by friends, he had not been entirely dependent on the presence of God for company and reassurance. He had accepted the sentiment of God's promise, "My presence shall go with thee"; but now God was facing him, not with the shadow of a theological statement, but with the practical experience of the presence of God. In the loneliness of that fog-blackened night, he acquired a confidence in the sufficiency of the divine presence to fortify his natural helplessness. His confidence was not just for that moment on a mountain trail to the Ilaga Valley but for future emergency in a missionary life stripped of former securities. At peace now with his lot, he drifted into slumber, finding the dripping trees no longer an irritation but a lullaby.

The next day two Danis travelling to Ilaga overtook them, and with the abrupt approach of the Papuans told them, "Back there where you stopped to eat yesterday our friend died."

"Died?"

"Yes, he slipped. The soft ground caved in and a stake speared him."

Dave Cole's eyes questioned him. He hoped it was an accident. They had entered a valley like a volcano crater, ringed with mountains. It reminded him of a stage set for a western film. From behind crevices a sudden charge of bandits with six-shooters cracking from their hips would not have appeared out of place. If evil men had a foul deed to commit, here was the storybook location.

Entering deep into the valley the party searched for the old trail. Mist swirled around them. Their feet sank into deep moss. Knotted with a cramp of fear, the carriers felt that with every step they would slip down into the river rumbling in some underworld below. They huddled together over a hole falling deep into bottomless darkness, whispering, "Don't look, dead man down there. Dead man down there."

The fog moved in to cover them and the wind wailed through the trees like a funeral dirge over the background of blanketed silence. "Don't be afraid, boys, God is with us. Stay close to us," Cole reassured them.

And the Danis stuck to them like their Siamese twins through the rest of the valley.

Out in the open, straddling a bridge high over a raging torrent, with a feeling of helplessness Cole knew that one misplaced step could take a man to his death. He thought of the Dani who had spent his life in these conditions, now dead on the trail. He gave thanks that they, the inexperienced, had come through.

At Ilaga the men picked up the generator and some advice from the local Danis which shortened the homeward trek but did not eliminate the cold walk over the pass. After two hours in a chilling downpour, they felt that they had reached their limit. With still another hour to the only shelter, the overhanging rock on the homeward side of the pass, the will took over the spontaneous actions of their bodies, forcing them on. Somehow their numbed fingers lit a fire from dry wood left in the shelter—a code of the Papuan trail. In the misery-dispelling warmth of its blaze, their spirits reached out, beyond their own resources, to the source of their inner strength.

11

Payback

ON THEIR RETURN to Mulia, Cole and Dillinger found encouraging progress being made on the strip by the men returned from the Sinac. These warriors who had gone to feast at the Sinac proved to be the pick of the Mulia males, with less outward effect from the valley's disease. They soon turned the flat area wedged between two mountain ranges into an airstrip.

To the MAF pilot, used to flying over the mountains, the four-day walk to make the routine preopening examination of the strip was agony. On arrival, dragging blistered feet but knowing that the men waited to hear his assessment of their work, he walked over the strip, measuring the softness and calculating the roughness.

"It's still very rough, the loose stones could be a hazard, and it needs to settle some more," he judged. "But if the airplane touches here," he said indicating an area, "it should be all right."

The men ripped up magazines and marked the touch down area with the pages. The Cessna came in and landed safely. As it flew out again, the pilot looked down through the window and was happy almost to tears. Now he could bring in a real stove to replace the one fashioned from a cut off benzine drum. The missionaries could have bedding instead of sleeping bags, mail and fresh meat to improve their living, and typewriters and duplicators to aid their work. And, of course the wives could come in. The little yellow airplane had become part of another team.

With the coming of the missionary wives to Mulia, more

AIRSTRIP MARKERS. Magazines were ripped up and used to mark the touchdown area at the new Mulia airstrip.

Dani women ventured onto the station. Sundays became the day that husbands took their families to the "zoo" to see the cat, dog, goat—and the missionaries.

Dina Cole, breastfeeding baby Larry, could scarcely screen herself from eyes prying through the cracks in the walls of her bush home.

Previously only one Mulia woman had come to the compound, and she came like a fireball of fury. Fear of the white man seemed to have left her completely this day. Charging after a Dani man, she caught and clouted him on the head while lashing him with her tongue. The astonished white spectators asked among themselves, "Is this just a normal domestic difference? Or has this fellow said his mother-in-law's name?" Saying the mother-in-law's name is as good as calling her a harlot and gives his wife cause to take a stick to him. Most men, in fear of the threat of growing prematurely old for doing so, did not insult their in-laws.

Such easily provoked tempers quickly dispelled the picnic

atmosphere, and not many of those early Sundays passed peace-
fully. On one of these days, a suitor dragged his screaming
girlfriend by the hair of her head past the missionary houses.
The more she protested, the more he kicked her. Maynard
grabbed and forced him to drop the rock which he had picked
up.

"Let her go," demanded Maynard. "You wouldn't do that
to your pigs."

When the bride buyer rushed off to his hamlet, Maynard,
certain that he would return with a bow and arrow, withdrew
to his house.

On occasions, the Danis too found the missionaries' house a
refuge. One afternoon Apbuluk, like the piper's son with a
pig under his arm, came running past Maynard who was working in front of his house. Three men, with arrows at the ready,
raced after him. The man out front turned side on, stretching
his torso to its narrowest to protect his vitals from the volley
of arrows. Unhit, he ran on. Another closely aimed shaft struck
Maynard's house above Apbuluk's head and broke off. Then
the pursued was gone. Nonplussed, his attackers searched
around the houses, in the outhouse, and among the bushes.

Maynard pushed his kitchen door to open it, but it jammed
against him. The wanted man had slipped in there. Not wanting murder on his doorstep, Maynard let Apbuluk hide until
his attackers, now arguing among themselves, went off.

Continued association with deformed idiots and no visible
impact on unresponsive minds brought frustration and deep
depression to the missionaries. At a low ebb, Ralph Maynard
was ready to say to his Master, "Lord, if this is your will, I
don't want it. I don't want to dissipate my life among these
objects."

He found it difficult to think of them as people, but as something somewhere between the human and the animal.

"Lord, wouldn't it be better if we pulled out of here and
went where we could expend our energies more profitably?"
he reasoned.

Then Maynard asked himself, "Does being born to an appreciation of refined living, care of the body, and an ability to develop knowledge exempt me from a responsibility to a handicapped fellow man?"

When a man who looks to God reaches the end of his own limits, God steps in and works a miracle. When many felt that there was no hope for the Mulia cretins, God transformed them into creatures worthy of His name.

Meanwhile, the missionaries, inspired by the hope of that miracle, worked on in the face of the absurd.

Although the Mulias soon understood that the missionaries' needle, jars of ointment, and pills could heal their wounds and diseases, they still made sacrifices to the spirits. Some of their rites were not to effect a cure so much as to ward off sickness and accident. They were to appease the spirits that the pressure of vindication might be eased.

Every so often they held such a ceremony when thousands gathered at a given place. The chiefs carried pigs, bound to poles, around the circumference of the crowd. Then as the animals were arrowed in the heart, the blood was caught in banana leaves as a sacrifice. The day following such a ceremony a big chief, miserable with toothache, came to Ralph Maynard.

"You had all that sacrificing yesterday, all that pig's blood, and here the very next day you have the toothache," Maynard gently reminded him.

The chief had no answer.

He had not long gone with his aching tooth and aspirin, when Eokkam, who had been a leader in the ceremony, came up looking very distressed.

"Hullo Eokkam, what's the matter?"

"Oh—h, I've an awful pain in my stomach."

"A pain! You ate so much pork at yesterday's feast that you have a stomachache? The very thing that was to stop pain has caused it!"

"Oh—h, give me a pill, Tuan. We know that the pig's blood is not strong, but what else can we do? We don't know what to do."

Sympathy towards their suffering and practical help in their illnesses won the confidence of the disease-ridden Mulias. Every mother knew the agony of giving birth to a dying child. Of every ten born, nine died. Eight women out of every ten ran the risk of giving birth to a cretin.

Although the missionary nurses reduced the mortality rate, they could not prevent the birth of deaf mutes and imbeciles. A plea to the Dutch government brought help.

Dr. Van Rijne was sent in by the Dutch government followed by a team from the Leiden University, in cooperation with the Rockefeller Research Institute to investigate the disease. Dr. Durupe, who visited Mulia in 1962, not only specialized in the study of goiter but also had a longstanding interest in the Danis. He was one of the few who had succeeded in penetrating the interior on foot. For twenty-six months, without any contact with civilization, he had lived in the interior. From his experience he said, "Without a doubt this is the most concentrated goiter pocket in the world."

Exhaustive tests were made, indicating iodine deficiency to be the major cause of the disease. As long as the mothers took iodine, no mentally retarded babies were born. Iodine injections shrank the mammoth goiters. A new hope had come to the people.

At the same time that medical science had begun to improve the Mulia's health, a spiritual movement was stirring the western Danis, bringing hope of the return of eternal life lost to them in the unremembered past. Ever since the missionaries had first told the Danis that at the time a man commits himself by faith to Jesus Christ, His life enters into that man and continues on after death, they had connected this teaching with their old legend about the snake and the bird. When Melba Maynard had stepped off the Cessna on one of the first flights into Mulia, Ralph heard a hoarse incredulous whisper behind him, "She's not a snake. We thought that the white man's wife was a snake!"

This comment stemmed from the confusion of their ancient beliefs about everlasting life with the Christian gospel. Native doctrines, closed to the outsider through lack of communication and fear, must first be understood by the missionary, so that he doesn't find himself presenting the gospel in a way which arouses cultural barriers in the hearer. From his treasury he draws "things old and new." The principle which he presents is old and changeless, but the application of it must ever be new, continually adapted to the persons about to receive it.

Inevitably it is the gospel itself which probes the darkened concepts and breaks them open to its purifying and educating light. The study of anthropology and linguistics are valuable aids in presenting the gospel of Jesus Christ, but it is only the entrance of the Word of God that gives light. The gospel is reflected light going from the instructed back to the instructor. As the missionary "gossips the gospel," the indigene reveals the barriers in his religion against which the new teaching is hitting, thus giving his teacher insight into his cultural problems. To a Dani who has no understanding of love, in the initial approach the love of God means nothing; but to a man bereft of eternal life, God's gift of this life was good news.

So that the missionary can understand the native thinking, top priority is given to the mastering of the local dialect. Mulia Dani, a seven-vowel language, is nearer the center of Western Dani than the five-vowel Bokondini dialect. A thorough word check showed ninety-five per cent similarity in the vocabulary of the western Dani dialects. Their grammatical construction was the same. This means that all missions were trying to crack the same linguistic problems.

To help solve these problems, intermission linguistic conferences were held regularly and attended by two or three delegates from each society in the Dani-speaking districts. A common orthography, agreed upon by these conferences, standardized the Dani literature. As knowledge of the language increased, portions of Scripture were designated to members of each society for translation.

To identify non-English sounds, reduce an unwritten language to writing, unravel its complex grammar, and then to converse in the idiom of the people is no mean feat. Any natural linguist was a welcome asset to the mission staff. David Scovill fitted right into the linguistic program.

Scovill and his wife Esther, daughter of missionaries working in Haiti, and both Prairie Bible School graduates, were greeted on the Mulia airstrip in September 1960 by the Maynards and a mob of pig-greased Danis. As Dave eased his bulk out of the plane, a voice rose from the crowd, *"Iyi, ap etti gwok* [Wow, he's a big man]!"

The Scovills' hours of disciplined language study were rewarded. Dave was preaching a limited message in less than two months, as well as pulling teeth and building houses. Raising rabbits and trying to hatch chickens in an improvised incubator, rigged to the chimney of his kerosene refrigerator, to furnish his own table as well as to improve Dani diet, were other outlets of his indefatigable energies.

Esther shut her eyes to fastidious housekeeping and let Watlumpak, one of the local boys, take over while she concentrated on language study, interspersed with helping out in the maternity block. One day while the tape recorder played back Dani words, she attended to some necessary kitchen chores. Watlumpak, washing dishes, picked up the word *forever.*

"Nonja, does God live forever?" he asked.

"Yes, He lives forever," Esther answered, "and I will live forever with Him."

"Will I live forever too?" the boy asked, looking to her for a satisfying answer. How could she qualify the 'yes' and 'no' in an honest answer within her language limit?

"When I know more of your talk, I will tell you," was all she could say.

The need was a continual goad to language study.

Because of regular afternoon rains, the houseboys left early each day, not returning until after breakfast the next morning.

"If we built a house for you right near ours, you could sleep there. Then you wouldn't need to go home each night," Scovill told Watlumpak.

"Oh, no, we couldn't sleep there," the boy protested. "The

woman, Kwewatnakwe, would come in the night and sprinkle poison on us. We would wake, knowing some evil was about."

Clutching his stomach and rolling in mock agony, he continued, "A terrible pain would seize our stomachs, they would bloat like this"—his spread fingers indicating a huge size—"and then we would die."

"Esther," said Dave, "Let's not be occupied with peripheral things, but keep to the main task. We must learn these boys' language, so we can tell them the truth that will free them from this fear."

They maintained this standard of their missionary life, with the result that the Scovills made a very worthwhile contribution to the linguistic program and a real impact upon the Danis.

The big chiefs from the southern mountains often visited the Mulia Valley with all the privileges of honored friends. A few weeks after the Scovills arrived, the mountain people came down to feast with the Mulias.

Women dug potatoes while men heated flat stones in long shallow drains, until they cracked and spat off chips of flint. When pits were dug and lined with grass and leaves, each man and boy contributing his armful, the men picked up the heated stones with long wooden tongs and interlined the pits over the grass. They placed more grass over the stones to protect the food from direct contact with hot stones. Then they threw in potatoes, corn, beans, and cucumbers, covered them with grass, piled on more heated stones and let them steam to perfection in the moisture from the foliage.

In the lull while the pits steamed like so many tiny volcanoes, somebody stood up and harangued the guests about a pig payment which had not been made. Men grabbed bows and arrows, and women scattered. A spokesman from each group strode to the center. They punctuated their impassioned speeches with threatening rattling of arrows.

When both sides returned to their places, still shouting, at a given signal they let fly a volley of hundreds of arrows. Just the one volley was fired. Only nine people were hit—five on

COWRIE SHELLS. Cowrie shells came to the Dani through elaborate and unknown routes. Although used as currency, the value of the shell lay in the social and ceremonial sphere, rather than in economics.

MEMORY WORK. Ralph Maynard teaches a Bible verse to a Dani.

one side, four on the other. Then the visitors fled for home
while the cooking pits steamed unopened.

This was the severing of diplomatic relations between the
two groups. The old standing of friendship had been removed.
Now anyone crossing the border faced the risk of an arrow. A
boy about twelve years old came over from the mountain group
to visit with Mulia relatives. Men of war, decorated and
feathered for butchery, filled his unprotected body with barbed
arrows while he slept with friends. This ignited a two-month
war ending in ruthless carnage.

The mountain people pushed the Mulias to the end of the
valley taunting them. "Now, how will you Mulias get us?
There are no trails, no bridges out."

But the Mulias went way out into a back valley, came
around and drove the mountain dwellers to a steep cliff edge.
Returning victorious they bragged to the missionaries. "We
pushed them over the cliff until there were none left."

"None at all left?"

"Only a handful. We killed them—men, women, girls, and
little boys like that," pointing to two-year old Timothy Maynard.

"You killed women and children?"

"Tuan, you don't understand. Women give birth to fighting
men—boys grow into warriors. Kill them all."

The missionaries had preached a positive gospel, not a list
of prohibitions. They believed that when the Danis accepted
the gospel, under the guidance of the Holy Spirit much that
was unworthy in their culture would be shown to them. But,
at their gloating recapitulation of merciless murder, Maynard's
wrath exploded.

"You men, you are rotten through and through. God is angry
with your sin, your foul killings, and your pride in victory.
If you do not leave it, He will cut you down."

The men shrugged, "Listen to him! He just doesn't understand payback."

With blazing eyes Maynard looked at them. Pity struggled
with disgust. He marveled at a God who could hate this in-

human slaughter and yet love these men in whose minds it had
been conceived. This was the love that had brought the Son
of God to redeem men. It was this same love, poured into
Maynard's heart, that had brought him to that valley of castoffs and would keep him there until Christ had been formed
in these Dani murderers.

Following hard on this heartless massacre, mixed-up reports
from the C&MA station at Ilaga came through to Mulia.
Mulias, who had quarried green stone from the cave in the
valley and traded it over the mountains to Ilaga, came back
with excited stories. Ilaga visitors brought the same reports.

"The Ilaga people are burning their fetishes."

"They say burn your fetishes and you'll get life without
end."

"Burn the fetishes, say the prayers, repeat the Scripture
verses, stop wars, don't steal, and you'll get *nabelan kabelan*—
that's what they are saying over at the Ilaga. Tuan, shall we
burn our fetishes and go on living forever, too?"

By the time the reports reached Mulia, they were a mixed-up
jargon of a little truth and much superstition and legality.
There was no conviction of sin, just a craze to get everlasting
life mixed up with thoughts of the present body going on forever with complete freedom from sickness.

"Don't have anything to do with it," cautioned Maynard,
afraid of a mass movement without any meaning.

"When you know more. When we know your language better and have instructed you in God's word then you can decide
what to do. Don't just do what other people are doing—wait
until God speaks to you."

The missionaries were fearful that the excitable and impul-
sive Danis, so closely knit by tribal ties, would rush headlong
into a movement which would be more difficult to correct than
converting them from paganism.

How were they to know, at this stage, that this was the begin-
nings of a tremendous movement involving the whole of the
western Dani?

12

Burning the Old Way of Life

THE ROAR of a great crowd rose on the wave of excitement. Frenzied dancers streamed down the main tracks to the open ground beyond the Bokondini mission station to join the hundreds of Danis already gathered.

Scores of men wore the everyday string skullcap, or the mop cap made from bark beaten until soft and rubbed black with pig fat and soot. Everyone who held any significant position in the clan was greased and feathered. Scarlet, jade, yellow, and blue feathers backed with bark, were tied around the matted hair of a sinewy father. To these he had added white fluffy breast-feathers fixed in a pompon on mud set ringlets. Someone had tied a red bandana around his ears and set his plumes on top. White and gold cockatoo feathers, like a misplaced halo, framed an evil face. Fight leader Eragayam added sunglasses to his naked splendor. Foot-long plumes danced to the animated speech of their wearers. Colored wreaths crowned young heads. Women had slung their best colored string-bags from their heads.

Yukwanak, chief of the Bokos, and old Eagle, the big man of the Bilus, marshaled their groups. The people squatted on their haunches. Every soot-encircled eye turned expectantly as Watnipbo, spectacular in a display of feathers, rose to his feet in the midst of the rumbling, swaying mass. He raised his hands high above his head.

"We'll pray," he said.

An uncanny stillness descended on the crowd. Watnipbo began to pray. And then, as if to impress God with the speed of his oratory, his praying gathered momentum and volume.

One of his henchmen moved among the crowd and any with
an open eye he tapped on the head, to teach him the ritual of
prayer.

The prayer concluded, Watnipbo proceeded with the main
theme.

Leaping about, he proclaimed the reason of the gathering.
Never before had a Dani held such an audience. The great
crowd inspired every latent sense of showmanship.

"Hear, you men of Bokondini! I, Watnipbo and these my
friends, have come from Ilaga to tell you how to get everlasting
life. The children of Bok have returned to restore to us the
immortality lost to us in the days of our fathers. This is what
they are doing in the Ilaga. This is how they are getting eternal
life."

The crowd waited.

"They are burning their fetishes. You must burn your *kukuwaks*, too, and live forever."

The crowd let go in a roar of approval.

Then, one after another, Watnipbo and his men awed the
crowd with Bible story after distorted Bible story told with
velocity and flourish. He impressed upon them that anything
with a green leaf was not to be picked on Sundays; certain
types of sweet potatoes were not to be eaten; they must not
climb over fences; if they dropped anything they must not
pick it up; no food or drink was to be taken before the Sunday
service.

At the conclusion of his address, the crowd streamed off to
the springs to quench their thirst. They had worked, danced,
and sat for four hours in the heat of the mountain sun, but no
one dared to break the fast from food and drink that Watnipbo
had previously proclaimed. Babies cried, but every mother
had been afraid to give her child the breast. Now they gorged
until the skin stretched across their distended stomachs.

Cooking pits were opened and the people ate the *inikinik* or
praise feast. Then the sick came. Watnipbo laid his hands on
the diseased and assured them of healing and the removal of
evil spirits. Long strings of cowrie shells were paid out for this

service. Then, well fed and with a tin full of cowrie shells and a new wife picked up on the way, Watnipbo and his troupe moved on to the next center.

The dismayed missionaries, feeling like a small barrage in the path of a tidal wave, watched the proceedings. Their apprehension grew as similar visitors from other areas drifted through. Each brought a different corruption of the same story —"burn fetishes, get eternal life."

The locals talked consistently of the same theme: "Burn fetishes—get eternal life."

Taboos mounted. Because bows and arrows were used for killing, they were classed as evil things and not to be used at all. As a result, all hunting of possums, pigs, and even rats ceased. Whenever food was taken, even a small piece of fruit, long ostentatious prayers were said. The Danis had merely added more devilry to their old culture.

As Garnet Ericson and Bert Power saw the Danis, without rational thought jumping from one wrong conclusion to another and being bound by a new legality, they reasoned with them.

"This is not the way to get eternal life. It is a gift from God, given to those who accept Jesus Christ, His Son as their substitutionary offering for sin. You cannot get it by doing all these things."

"General Mac," who had organized the missionaries' carrier line from Kelila when they had first entered the Boko Valley, pushed all before him.

"Tuan," he answered, "You don't know. The true words have been given to the Ilaga people. They have got the right message. This is what they have told us to do, and this is what we shall do."

Knowing that this was not the "true word" that had been given out at Ilaga, Ericson and Power, in conjunction with the other missions, invited Gordon Larson, the C&MA missionary at Ilaga, to visit their stations and contradict this heresy by giving the true teaching. As far as the Danis were concerned, this new doctrine had begun at Ilaga. C&MA had built an airstrip and begun mission work in the Ilaga Valley in the western boundaries of the Dani population. Some Uhundunis, from south of the Carstenz Range had migrated to the area two generations previously and taken up residence in the remote valleys. Although the Danis despised the insignificant Uhundunis, there had been some intermarriage between the two tribes.

The Uhundunis had a myth that an improved way of life, called *hai* would suddenly come to their society. The Ilaga segment of the tribe saw the fulfilment of their long awaited *hai* in the coming of the missionary with his abundance of shell, steel, and talk of peace. Because, in the Papuan thinking, no one acts as an individual, this new teaching was accepted by the whole group.

Under pressure of a Roman Catholic priest, some of the Uhundunis in the main body of the tribe in the South had burnt their fetishes. Reports of this came through to the Ilaga Uhundunis. After long discussions they decided to burn their fetishes, too.

Through family relationships between the two tribes, Dani chief Opalalok, father-in-law of one of the leading Uhunduni Christians, instead of jeering at the gospel, as his fellow-clansmen did, began to think seriously about the effect that it had made upon his neighbors. Opalalok questioned his missionary about the results if ceremonies, dependent upon these fetishes, were abandoned. Receiving satisfactory answers the chief steeled himself against the public opinion, the wrath of angry spirits, and declared his faith in Christ to protect him.

At the end of 1958, at Opalalok's hamlet the first western Danis burnt their fetishes, the symbols of their old life, and looked by faith to a new way. Other villages followed. By the end of 1960 most of the Ilaga Danis had set fire to their ceremonial charms.

To cope with the teaching of these new candidates for Christianity, Gordon Larson established a "witness school." Married couples who had spiritual perception and leadership ability were appointed by their district to come into the Ilaga station

for concentrated instruction. For certain days of the week they
were taught from the Scriptures. Then they returned to their
villages to repeat what they had learned. The further from
the source, however, the more distorted the teaching became.
Villagers repeated their jumbled impressions of what they
thought had been said. These misconceptions spread from
hamlet to hamlet. Insignificant factors in Bible stories took on
disproportionate importance. Taboos grew out of the teaching.
Traders in and out of Ilaga took out garbled reports.

In areas outside regular mission contact, and therefore with
no adequate follow-up, rumors and false interpretations multi-
plied. "Prophets" like Watnipbo, men with ability to hold and
sway crowds with their verbosity, rose up among these fringe
groups. They in turn canvassed other areas until a vast amount
of talking was being done by ill informed men with an eye to
profit.

Appalled by the tales which were coming through, and
believing that God could not be in a movement which was
giving birth to falsehood, the missionaries tried to stem its
spread. The fire, having taken hold of the Dani mind, could
not be quenched. Fanned by the belief that they would gain
eternal life according to their legend, news blazed through
the valleys. Competition for prestige between paternal groups
pressured headmen to follow others in burning their fetishes.

Danis closest to the missionaries, and who had accepted their
teaching as truth but had not as yet grasped its import, came
to them for advice and accepted their explanations. But the
vast hordes away from the center of teaching were insistent
that their message had come from Ilaga, the birth place of the
"true talk." Even the faithful were being influenced by this
hard talking and were confused as to where the truth lay.
Gordon Larson accepted the invitation of the three areas most
affected by this false teaching and with two of his leading witness school men, Jubit and Jyybittu, made an overland trek
through these areas.

Thousands gathered at every center to hear the truth about
getting everlasting life. At Bokondini Gordon Larson and

Garnet Ericson sat with the crowds while Jubit and Jyybittu told what they had learned and experienced at Ilaga. They denied the rumors and taboos that had mushroomed through the valleys. When Larson could see that some point was not clear to the intently listening crowd, he arose and explained it until it was fully grasped. The Danis accepted the explanations and realized that their local missionaries were giving them this same teaching. They could see, too, that in the doctrines of Jesus Christ lay the secret of eternal life. This tied in with their legend which said that one day the descendants of their ancestor Bok would return from the west and restore to them their lost life. The missionaries had come from the west bringing this message and so were obviously the awaited descendants. All this was within the traditions of their fathers and could be accepted.

However, they were still convinced that their fetishes must go. At this stage there was no conviction of sin, no remorse for evil deeds committed, no acknowledgment of Jesus Christ as Saviour. They wanted that which they had lost. There was still confused conviction in many minds that their mortal bodies would be freed from sickness and take on immortality. Because of this, the missionaries questioned the worth of fetish burning without a change of heart.

Along with the exhortation to burn the *kukuwaks* had been the injunction to give up fighting and dancing and to stop stealing and lying. The missionaries were against a moral reform without an inner power to keep the changed way of life consistent. They knew that an attempt by the Danis to live by a golden rule, without the Holy Spirit working within, could result in a devastating lapse. Such a failure could turn the Danis against Christianity and could cause them to condemn it as unworkable. Therefore, the missionaries reasoned with the people to give serious thought to these things but not to burn their fetishes until they knew more of the teaching of Jesus Christ.

"How can we learn God's Word while we have these charms?

How can we hear God's Word while the spirits of our fathers are talking to us?" the Danis argued.

Old Eagle, chief of the Mbilu tribe, filthy of body, foul of speech, debated, "God can see all and knows what is going on. We can't do anything that's hidden. We are afraid. We want to get completely rid of these things and follow after God."

"While we have the *kukuwaks* we are thinking of them instead of the things of God," explained Kaniweyanak. "We are tied up with these things. They completely entangle us, so that we cannot take hold of the things of God."

"Before we can start to get God's way straight we must get loose from these bonds," they all agreed. "Burning is the only way in which we can be freed forever from them."

After two days of debating with the Danis, the missionaries could see that not only were they determined to burn, but that there could be no place for laying a foundation of Christian teaching while they were wrapped up in spirit worship.

Although the gospel of Christ demands individual appropriation, in a society where religious paraphernalia was community owned and each person functioned as a significant part of the group, group acceptance of Christianity is sometimes necessary before individual accounting with Christ can be effective. The missionaries, concluding that this was the pattern that the Dani society would take, did not hinder the burnings but continued to press the claims of Christ upon the individual.

Each mission station in the western district was experiencing this same excited interest in the gospel. It was ten to twelve months later that ten Mulia chiefs came to Maynard and Scovill to discuss their proposed plans for burning fetishes in their area.

"We'll make a fire on the airstrip right after the morning service on Sunday," they explained.

At ten o'clock the crowd started to move in. For four hours fifteen hundred singing and dancing Danis gathered from every valley and mountain village. The great crowd had washed their bodies and hair. Men had even scrubbed their pubic gourds, and the women their string bags. This voluntary bathing was unique to the Mulia burnings.

"I don't know for how many centuries these people have been tucked away in these mountains, but I guess this is the first bath that most have known," Mel Maynard observed to her husband. "It's certainly pleasant not to have soot and grease rubbing off onto us."

By two o'clock, the missionaries, who had scarcely noticed that they had missed their Sunday dinner, had the crowd seated. The service finished, a group went to get wood for the fire. With logs held high above their heads and singing as they came, they charged up the airstrip.

The great crowd separated into companies. A leader standing alone near the wood laid for the fire, held out a split stick. Half a dozen men came in turn from each of the companies and inserted small bone daggers, pigs' trotters, and a piece of dried-up human flesh into the split in the stick. When the leader had placed these prized heirlooms on the firewood, another chief, flanked by two men, stepped forward and stood by the logs. After a few moments' pause he laid a spear and several bows and arrows beside the split stick.

With the placing of these first articles upon the pyre the Danis surged forward. Score upon score came with something to burn. Bows, arrows, spears, stone axes, stone and bone knives, fur and feather headdresses, pigs' tails, nose bones, bridal stones, armbands, necklaces, ornamental shells, pieces of cane, and bits of this and that. Each item represented some function or history in their life. Each article was in some way directly related to the spirits, such as the blue-black cassowary plumes bundled together to make a "feather duster" and waved to chase away evil spirits.

Even the sorceresses came. One a hard, tough old woman with skin of wrinkled leather, seemed to be the chieftainess of her kind. Filthy and evil smelling, with bones jangling around her neck, she had taken her first bath and laid her pigs' tails and magic charms on the mountain of fetishes. As the women surrendered their media of witchcraft, the men cheered.

FETISH BURNING. Fetishes were burned to indicate the break with the old superstitions.

Chief Alumarek-lek stood on the logs by the pile of mounting fetishes. He took off his headdress, his beads, shell, and armbands of desiccated animal entrails rubbed smooth with years of greasy handling, and flung them down. He took out a bone dagger stained with his victims' blood, "With this I've killed ten men"; and he spat on it and threw it onto the pile.

The old chief was not the only one who spat. Men and women used their spittle freely to bid their bondage good riddance. Some, who had nothing else to throw on the heap, came again to spit and hiss.

"They'll be lucky to get the thing to burn with all that moisture about," Maynard commented.

The big rush subsided. A few, who had second thoughts concerning some adornment, rushed out and before they changed their minds again, tore off the trinket, said harsh words over it, and threw it with defiance onto the pile.

The Danis had been cautioned not to burn just for burning's sake, but to get rid only of the things connected with the spirits. An old man had been overheard in conversation with another as he fingered the shell beads around his boy's neck.

"This one we'll burn—it's a spirit thing. This one and this one and this one are nothing. These we'll keep. This and this and this are spirit. They will burn."

Some had been encouraged by others to burn certain objects, as Ralph Maynard himself had been.

"Tuan, you must burn your fetishes too."

Maynard looked baffled, "I haven't any fetishes," he said. "Oh, yes, you have. Those arrows in the closet in the top of your house. Those which you bought from the fellows over the hill."

Maynard had forgotten all about those arrows, but now he remembered and he very much wanted to keep them as souvenirs.

"But I am not going to use them as *kukuwaks*. They will just stay there locked in the cupboard," he explained.

"No Tuan, they are fighting things dedicated to the spirits. You should burn them," they urged.

Maynard told himself that if they were going to be an offence to the people they must go. Somewhat reluctantly, and knowing that he would never again be able to purchase such a souvenir, he went and got them and cast them on the pyre with the others. He didn't know whether to be sorry that he had not already sent them off to America or be glad that he could identify with the people. He decided to be glad.

The last fetish was laid on the pyre. The people sat on the grass waiting for the firing. Atlumarek-lek and the chiefs looked at Maynard. Ralph nodded at them. "Are you going to light it now?"

"Tuan, you are to light it."

"No," said Maynard, "This is your responsibility. These are your things. The burning is your idea. We don't want you to say later, 'The missionaries burned our fetishes.' "

"Oh, no, Tuan. We will never say that."

"But you might. It's your place to burn your *kukuwaks.*"

Maybe some fear of evil retaliation, if of their own volition they set light to this mountain of charms and destroyed all it represented, held them back.

For half an hour they argued back and forth.

At last Maynard compromised, "Look, we'll do it together."

The chief appointed came forward with a bunch of grass. Maynard put a match to it. Atlumarek-lek put the blazing grass under the firewood. Smoke seeped out under the logs. The flames from the grass made darting tentative licks at the kindling and, liking what it tasted, roared to devour it. The age-old fetishes, tinder-dry and some crumbling with age, were enveloped in fire. The great crowd watched the objects curling and twisting as though in anguish in the heat of the inferno.

This was no attic cleaning of unwanted junk. Each object had been a vital part of the owner's life. This was no raking up and autumnal burning of fallen leaves. Each man and woman had deliberately burnt the symbols of the only way of life that he and she had ever known. Although they had purposefully destroyed the power behind their former lives to make room for a better way, some looked at the irreparable destruction with a question throbbing in their minds about the unknown way ahead.

Nevertheless many were like old Atlumarek-lek, who had burned so much. Standing stripped of his former glory he watched the fire die down, the symbols of his leadership and priesthood now ashes in the glowing coals. He let out a long breath.

"My heart is happy, very happy," he said.

On the next Sunday another three thousand gathered. Some from far off had heard about the burnings and had come to destroy their fetishes too. Others had been present on the previous Sunday, but had not been able to bring themselves to burn all. But now the presence of those unburied symbols

so troubled them that they came to rid themselves of everything.

On the third Sunday another great burning took place, when
folk from other valleys joined the Dani congregation on the
airstrip. They too burned their fetishes.

Each Sunday hundreds came to hear the teaching about the
new way into which they had entered. After every service
some outlying areas had fetishes to burn. In the seventh week
after the first burning the chiefs came in to Maynard and
Scovill.

"We've finished the burnings and now we want to bury the
ashes."

On the following Wednesday another large concourse gathered to see the hole dug and the charred pile of the symbols
of centuries of demon worship consigned to it and covered
over—to be forgotten forever.

The chief brought in two pigs and invited Maynard to kill
them with a bow and arrow. Then they ate a pork-and-potato
"feast of happiness" to commemorate the burnings and their
start of a new way of life. Maynard remembered the time
before when Atlumarek-lek had arrowed a pig and caught its
blood to cajole the spirits to give them health and life. He
reminded him of it. The old man spat and wrinkled his nose.

"No good. No good at all," he said. "We didn't know any
better. Now our hearts are hungry for God."

With fetishes burnt in the Kelila, Bokondini, and Mulia
areas, the people swarmed into the stations to learn more of the
new life which they had embraced. Hundreds came every
Sunday and scores during the week.

Among them was Blackie, a chief from the Mulia area. His
matted hair hanging down to his waist was his great pride.
There were few his equal in dirt, sensuality, and filthy, lying
talk. He too burnt his fetishes and washed his body.

"Tuan, I have a very big garden to make," he said one morning to David Scovill. "When I have finished, I will come and
then you will teach me Bible verses too."

After several weeks he returned and fell into step beside

LONG HAIR. Blackie, a chief from the Mulia area, was very proud of his long, matted hair. He cut it after his conversion to show that he was finished with personal pride.

Scovill who with hammer and saw was returning home from the house which he was building.

"Today I finished my garden," Blackie said, bending his little finger into the palm of his hand. Flipping down the next finger, he continued. "On this day I will rest in my house." Then, taking hold of the middle finger, "On this one I'll come so that you can teach me."

"Will you come morning or afternoon?"

"If you have work for me, I shall come in the mornings and then in the afternoons we will learn the Word. But, tell me before I go, who was the white man's father way back at the beginning?"

"Adam."

"Who was his wife?"

"Eve."

"Who was Adam's father?"

"He didn't have a father. God created him."

Scovill told Blackie the story of the creation and fall of man. The chief, nodding his head, thought about this for some time. "Tell me again," he said, "What was that man's name that was made out of dirt?"

"Adam."

"Yes, that was the white man's father. Who was the black man's father?"

"That same Adam was father of both black and white."

Blackie stood digesting that fact.

"Here we are black; you are white. Before, we did not know this. You have come and told us. Because we have the same father, we have fellowship together."

Each day he came and would not leave until he had learned his Bible verse.

When Blackie burned his fetishes, he washed the dirt from his body and the grease from his hair. His hair, however, he kept long, a proud symbol of his position in his tribe.

Most evenings, before the Scovills had finished their evening meal, Blackie would come to squat on the floor beside them. While he ate the potato which had been kept for him, he asked questions about the message that had been preached on Sunday.

One evening as he took his potato he said, "Tell me about the girl who knew God."

"The girl who knew God? Whom does he mean?" the Scovills asked themselves.

"Oh, I know," said Esther. "The servant girl in the story of Naaman."

This man who was a general in his own tribe and had marshaled his troops against the enemy did not ask about the leprous warrior. A high priest in his own religious culture, he did not ask about the prophet who performed a miracle, but this seeker for God asked about the girl who had found Him. The missionaries told them how a man could know God.

Then Blackie's son sickened and died. The father was beside himself with grief.

He asked the Scovills, "I've burned all my fetishes; I've cleaned my heart; I've given up lying and stealing. Why has God let my son die?"

The missionary answered, "Only God can answer that. God is good. All He does is good. Just now we cannot understand why God took your boy. When we get to heaven, God will tell why. Now we accept His way as right."

The man was satisfied, calmed, and at peace. The next day at the cremation he prayed a prayer of acceptance of the will of God as perfect and beyond question. He had no need to make pig sacrifices or to divinate to find a sorceress responsible for the death.

While his son's body burned, Blackie cut off his long black hair. He had cut away the last of his pride.

"We used to be big men, but we are big no more," he said. "No man is important, not even the missionaries. Only God is big."

With the death of his son, Blackie had learned that the burning of fetishes did not give the earthly body immortality, but he had also learned that death did not separate a Christian from God. Neither did grief separate from God but rather

enlarged fellowship with Him. This was knowing God—the essence of eternal life that begins the moment a man commits
himself to God. All this Blackie had accepted through teaching from the Bible by the missionary and in the experience
of the death of his child.

But away in the valleys and hills were thousands who still
thought that because they had burned their fetishes their
bodies would not die nor know sickness. Because so many
like Blackie were coming, demanding teaching and answers
to their questions, Mulia, Bokondini, and Kelila were given
instruction classes. The missionaries called them witness
schools after the pattern of those already started in the Ilaga
Valley.

Because the burnings at Bokondini and Kelila had been
some months in advance of those at Mulia, their program was
that much further ahead. Time was the only factor which put
these two stations ahead of the dull-minded Mulias. With the
medication that the "cast offs" were receiving, and with the
release from fear and evil practices which the gospel had
brought, a keenness had come to their wits.

The three schools were built on the same foundations. Those
residing in a particular area nominated a married couple from
among them as their representative. These couples formed the
student body of the schools. The students, with the missionaries, agreed among themselves what regulations would exist.

They decided that none should live in any reported sin, and
that all must maintain a constant desire for Bible learning. A
man must be husband to one wife only. This ruling limited the
students to the younger age group; but as a consequence, the
schools would have the men and women with the better ca-
pacity for learning.

During classes the students lived in a village built near the
station. Although the missionaries suggested that this village
should follow the U-shaped pattern of paternal hamlets with
a *matno* or men's house at the head of the women's huts, by
their own consent the couples wished to live as man and wife
in their own houses. It was to be a model village where they

would learn hygiene and demonstrate to other villages the workability of cleanliness. No pigs were allowed in the houses but were fenced outside the village. Latrines were dug. Paths were laid and flowers grown.

During the week they learned the simple Bible stories and their practical applications. First, the Old Testament gave a foundation for the reason of their faith in Christ; and then later they delved into the New Testament for the life, work, and teaching of Christ to outline the ethics of Christian living.

On the weekends they returned to their own districts and passed on what they had learned. This was done in a conversational way around the hamlet fires. To prevent the confusion which had arisen at the beginning of the mass movement, preaching to large groups was not encouraged.

Reading and writing were included in the witness school curriculum for those who had not already learned to read in the literary classes. It was hoped that in the giving out of their lessons the students would enlarge and deepen the meaning of what they had learned, because of the fluency in their mother tongue and their understanding of their own people's need. This was not so. They learned the stories by rote and gave out nothing else.

During the day little groups huddled together in the villages, around the mission stations, and along the paths. At night they clustered around the fires. All were learning the writing on the paper. Every man and woman, young and old, said it over and over until he could repeat it back like a well-taught parrot.

They thought, "We have the Word. This will give us life." It was almost another fetish.

As yet the Danis knew nothing of the Holy Spirit and His guidance. They could express themselves only the way that they had known throughout the centuries: that a rite must be performed in an exact fashion to get the desired results. They looked for the import in an insignificant detail and imitated everything which the missionary did. To fail to perform in a like manner would bring retaliation from God. Prayer became

a new "taboo talk," and failure to shut the eyes during prayer
would result in blindness. Sitting in church would bring im-
munity from sickness. At the root of the cessation from stealing, lying, and other major vices was fear of retaliation from
God. Along with these reasons came the rite to commit the
Word of God to memory and to give it back with machine gun
rapidity. Because man has a built in drive to come to the top,
there was competition and pride in outquoting another, as
well as the urge for greater reward.

In the midst of all this was the compulsion to recover eternal life. The missionaries were afraid of a mass movement
without the power of the Holy Spirit. Therefore they exer-
cised the more care to restrain the movement, while at the
same time endeavoring not to restrict the freedom of the Holy
Spirit to operate sovereignly in each Dani.

At this stage while the witness school people confined themselves to miming only what was written on their papers, there
was no danger of error being propagated. Their inexhaustible
enthusiasm to learn the Word of God provided an unprecedented platform for proclaiming the gospel. The missionaries
made full use of the opportunity. They continued to fill the
water pots and prayed that the Holy Spirit would turn it into
wine.

Garnet Ericson wrote of the Bokondini situation to Charles
Horne, who was then in Australia on furlough.

> Their position is one of desiring the way of God and yet
> still held in the chains of their old life. They will tell me that
> they are straight, but generally, incidents tell a different story.
> They have no conviction of sin, which at this stage and with
> the speed of the movement is not surprising. But it adds to
> the realization that our need is to keep Bible teaching before
> them that the Holy Spirit may bring this conviction.
>
> One of the greatest problems is to get them to relate this
> teaching to themselves and not to the fellow next door. I think
> they have grasped that the burning of fetishes was not the
> end but the beginning. At present I am trying to make it
> plain to them that they have two choices:

1. The reception of Christ to be their strength in walking straight.
   or
2. The rejection of Christ's claims and its resultant divine judgment.

   Although they accept this with their emotions much teaching is necessary to show them Christ and their need of Him.

Three months later he wrote again, "I feel we have come to the position we have been awaiting."

At the time of the burning of their fetishes, the missionaries had persuaded the Bokondinis not to burn their weapons lest their enemies overrun them. During the months immediately following the burnings, the warriors debated the problem of their munitions. Some wanted to wait to see what their enemies would do; others felt that while they retained their arms their houses were only half cleaned. When the majority decided to burn, Ericson resolved to make an issue of it. He challenged them to cut completely away from evil spirits and to array themselves on the side of Christ, by not only burning their weapons, but by confessing their *amoluk kunik*.

"While the *amoluk kunik* is still in your hearts, there is no purpose in burning your weapons," he told them. "Christ wants heart surrender. He will not be deceived by hypocritical, showy display of burning bows, arrows, and spears while in your hearts you still keep what you consider is the power behind them."

The *amoluk kunik* seemed to be a power for revenge implanted in the heart of a warrior at the time of a certain sacrifice. A man mortally wounded in battle covered the fact of his wound to all but a close relation. When the wounded man died, the relation who alone knew the cause of his death, secretly killed a pig. Then he cut away that part of the pig's anatomy which corresponded with the wounded part of the dead man's body. When he had sacrificed it to the spirits, he ate it.

The spirit of the dead man blessed this relation by bestowing upon him the power to avenge his kinsman's death. The killers, ignorant that they were the cause of the man's death, were unaware that an impregnable force had been set against them. Those who had received the power of a dead man's spirit became *wakakget,* a driving force in battle. A group without *wakakget* men who have received the *amoluk kunik* is vulnerable to the enemy. When they become vulnerable, *toponak,* they turn tail and flee, believing that they have no chance of survival in a fight, although they may be numerically superior.

Not long after mission work began at Bokondini, the Omaka group became *toponak* and fled before their attackers, leaving their villages to be plundered and burnt. Many refugees were mercilessly slaughtered.

The power of the *amoluk kunik* lost its potential and the spell was broken once the recipient disclosed the name of the person from whom he had received it. So, if a Dani confessed his *amoluk kunik* to God, in his thinking he was putting himself into the hands of his enemies. Therefore, the Danis gave much consideration to this subject.

At a large meeting of several hundred, Garnet Ericson again challenged them. "If you give up your fighting and burn your weapons, and follow God, is it good for a man still to be living under the spell of an evil spirit? You cannot say, 'I shall still hold on to my *amoluk kunik* in case God's power does not work.' God won't tolerate that kind of bargaining. You come to God under His conditions. That is, you cut with everything to do with Satan and his lies and you trust God and Him only. Until you are ready to break the spell of the *amoluk kunik* you are not ready to burn your weapons. This is something which each one of you will have to think through and act upon for yourselves."

13

Chasing the Shadow

ON THEIR INITIAL TREK through to Mulia, the missionaries had paced the "table top" dropping into the plunging Nogolo and agreed, "this is enough for an airstrip! We'll center another witness here."

At the time that the Ilaga people were burning their fetishes and rumors were fanning out from there, Dave Cole and Austin Lockhart moved into Iluwagwi, commonly called Ilu, where the Nogolo, skirting the main divide, drained the Upper Rouffaer. Lockhart, a powerfully built football captain, while at college had heard an appeal for "red-blooded" Americans to evangelize West New Guinea. Adventure and rugged country had challenged his athlete's spirit; he and his little Kentucky wife, Laurie, packed up their belongings, collected an "outfit," and set sail via Australia for New Guinea.

Cole and Lockhart walked right into a major war in the Ilu valley. The local chief remembered that Cole was one of the men who had passed through Ilu to Mulia. He welcomed both men warmly but, being occupied with driving out the enemy, had no time to organize labor gangs for their airstrip work. Each morning Cole and Lockhart walked from the shack, hastily erected at the building site, while warriors formed for battle. Rubbing his thighs, with hands dug deep in his trouser pockets, Cole dropped the corners of his mouth.

"There goes the day's labor again," he said.

As the warriors charged past the two men, they called, "You stay there. No one will harm you. We're after the enemy."

The missionaries had not come to hide in a shack. They had work to do. Recruiting nine nonfighters they began to level off for the strip while rallying calls to battle, victory shouts, and cries of terror beat against their ears.

"If they would only expend some of that energy in helping us here, they'd be that much nearer finishing with wars," sighed Lockhart.

"I'll walk out to those Ilu villages to see if I can channel some of that manpower into giving us a hand," Dave Cole offered.

Entering into some light scrub he met a war party, blackened and belligerent. By sneaking along the outskirts of the local territory, this crowd from the western side of the range had purposed to meet and ally themselves with the enemy on the far side of the valley.

The lone missionary and the fighting force measured each other. Cole's dry humor broke through, and his face creased into smiles.

"Hi, you fellows! Are you looking for work?" he asked.

But without deigning to answer, the corps tossed their feathered heads and trotted off down the hill.

From a hilltop the two missionaries watched the alliance between the enemy and this new group. They counted five hundred houses which had been set alight by the united drive of these two groups. They saw the locals pushed right out of their country into the next valley. Many fatally wounded were hidden away so that the *amulok kunik* would become potent in another.

The missionaries exhausted their medicines in an attempt to meet the medical needs of the wounded and diseased. When called out to attend a man high up on a mountain trail, Cole came upon a miniature hut, as tiny as a doll's house. His interest was roused.

"Tell me what it is. I'm going to look at it."

"No, no. A little girl lives there."

"A little girl!"

As Cole moved toward the hut, Ap Poram's hand on his arm restrained him.

"No, no. Your eyes don't want to see that. Your nose doesn't want to smell it. It is a big smell. She has many sores."

Yaws, thought Dave, and strode towards the house.

He rapped on the door.

Two frail little hands fumbled at the wooden barriers that closed the doorway. A hot, nauseating stench breathed out from the house. Cole reeled back. Repulsion changed to pity welling in his chest, bruising his throat, at the sight of the little girl, eight years old, standing in the doorway looking questioningly up at him. At every joint a large sore ate into her flesh. Already part of the nose was gone and the carnivorous disease reached out to consume the eyes. Dave turned to his companion, "When we have slept for a man's two fists, we will have finished the airstrip, and the plane will come and bring medicines. Then we shall make this little one better." Ten days. The Danis counted time by the nights slept and reckoned in tens, counted by closed fists.

For days Dave Cole brooded over that little girl and the story of despair that her condition told. Because none, not even her mother, could live with the offensive smell, her people had built her a little house, daily brought food, firewood, and water and left her to rot. His heart rebelled against those who dared to say, "Let the heathen be. They are happy as they are."

Cole worked and waited for the medicine. When it came, the child was gone. The war flooding in had flushed out refugees, among whom were the little girl's people. They had taken her with them into the far valleys, but the missionaries did not see or hear of her again.

The Ilus, too, had caught smatterings of the talk about the return of eternal life to the Dani tribe. When the missionaries entered the Upper Rouffaer Valley, their origin was not questioned. They had already been established as the "givers of eternal life." Speculation over this new message mingled with warfare and domesticity.

"Tuan," a Poram said to Dave Cole, "My friend away up there on the mountain has the spirit pain. You come and see him."

"My friend, I have no medicine left."

"Never mind, you just come."

"But I can do nothing without medicine."

"It's all the same. You just come."

Yielding to his insistence, Dave Cole went with Ap Poram. As they neared his hamlet on the mountain top, a large crowd moved restlessly about the huts. When Cole clambered over the paling fence into the village compound, a sudden expectant silence fell. With extreme watchfulness the men stepped back and lined the path to let Cole and Ap Poram approach the house.

Cole stopped and followed the Dani into the hut. The patient lay in the center of the floor facing the door. Cole bent over him, then sat back drawing in his breath.

"Your friend is dead! You told me that he was sick."

The fellow squatting on his heels beside him grinned sheepishly.

"Yes, I know. But, you take him to your house and he will come alive again."

"But I can't do that."

"Oh, yes, you can. You are a friend of God's. Of course you can."

The others who had swarmed into the hut vehemently agreed with Ap Poram.

"Yes, yes. You can do this."

Cole pleaded with them that he could not do this, that they must burn their friend's body.

The Danis were shocked. They had heard that the missionary could raise the dead and had come expecting to witness the miracle.

The missionaries hurried into a preaching program to stem these rumors which were pouring into the area. But the rumors were louder than the preaching and continued to grow.

A man who had lost an eye in battle years before and now was totally blinded by a recent arrow was led again and again to the missionaries.

"You touch him. You just touch him and he will see."

At the funeral of a man accidentally killed while hunting cuscus (a small animal with an abdominal pouch) the people

increased offers of cowrie shells and finally a pig to new missionary, Stan Sadlier, to persuade him to give the dead man
life.

Seeing no grey hairs in the heads of the young missionaries,
the Danis were convinced that they had drunk the elixir of
eternal youth and that death could not touch them. To the
Dani thinking, men with such wisdom and authority could
not be young men.

A fellow who peered through the bedroom window and saw
Dina Cole in bed, laughed in unbelief that she was ill. When
Dave and Dina's new baby died at birth, however, they ac-
cepted the fact that white men experience death.

The missionaries continued the meetings, repeating the fundamental truths over and over again.

"But," the Danis said, "There is no point in our coming to
your meetings. While we have the spirit paraphernalia, our
ears are plugged. We must burn our fetishes."

They came in thousands, threw their stuff into the fire places,
and set light to it. As the flames leaped forty feet into the air,
the people turned and fled. They had finished with these
things but were afraid of reprisal.

They had turned from idols to serve the true and living God
without any knowledge of who He is or of how to serve Him.
Perhaps their sole desire was for the benefits which they
thought they could so obtain.

One, Papinggawe, the possessor of a white boar, (introduced
by the missionaries) rigged himself a "radio" from used powdered milk cans. In his house at Tenggen Ambut, halfway between Ilu and Mulia, he "listened in" and persuaded those
who would pay, that he had received the true words from God.

For a price, the owner of a sick pig could discover the
source of the sickness by pouring water over the white boar's
back. If it ran off in a certain way, the malady was caused
by spirits. For another payment Papinggawe would pray over
the water, caught as it poured off the pig's back, to effect a
cure. Those who would become Papinggawe's disciples were

permitted to breed their sows with the white boar to raise some magic for themselves.

The repetition of certain words, or appropriate blowing of tobacco smoke as instructed by the milk-tin radio, would acquire desired effects. Papinggawe published the "message" that God would send axes and knives down from heaven with the rain. Trading on the superstitious credulity of the people, he prepared a path for "cargo cultism."

Papinggawe went to Mulia expecting to propagate this perversion at the Sunday service. He was refused a platform. The next Sunday his followers met the Mulia witness school men, on their way to their usual preaching posts, with a shower of arrows.

The Danis, a people who had operated their lives according to omens, demanded a sign. Therefore, nonsense became wisdom, and the trivial urgent.

"Look into a tin can. If you can see that which is behind you reflected over your shoulder, well, that's Satan looking in at you. It's a sure sign that your heart's not right," they told each other.

Legalism carried over from former ritualism, and pharisaism, resulting from a compulsion to please the missionaries whom the Danis recognized as the media through whom God worked, dominated the Dani thinking. Every evening, two women on their way home from the potato gardens, paused by the missionary's gate and said long loud prayers to impress him with their piety.

Man can conceive an image of God only within the limits of his knowledge of Him. Because the Danis did not yet know God, they clothed Him in the likeness of the vindictive ruling spirits with which they were familiar. Cleanliness, sanitation, saying long prayers before eating a potato, and learning the Word of God were Dani-designated demands of God; and failure to conform would evoke His judgment.

The missionaries had told the Danis that poor sanitation was a major cause of epidemics and a preventative measure would be to build toilets. Their superstitious minds interpreted the advice this way: "The missionary is the mouthpiece of God, therefore this is a command from Him. Failure to build a little house behind the village will call forth the anger of God. He will retaliate by sending sickness."

It was imperative that in teaching, the missionary give only fundamental facts. The Dani mind would fix upon a nonessential detail and give it major significance until it, too, became a principle upon which to build one's life. This situation sometimes arose while a missionary, looking for a Dani expression, inadvertently focused attention on a minor point. In teaching the doctrine of the new birth, the story of Nicodemus coming to Jesus at night was told. With their earnestness to imitate every detail, Dani men, thinking that their soul's salvation hinged on a nocturnal visit, began coming after dark to talk with the missionaries. In some areas people began to speak only in whispers and ceased to reprimand their children in an exaggerated reaction to teaching against brawling, killing, and maiming.

In the same mood of this unbalanced gullibility, the Danis destroyed thousands of *yao* stones, the currency for the purchase of brides and pigs. These stones were the Danis' most valued possession. At that time, one stone was worth a month's wages.

Fearing an economic depression, the missionaries pleaded against it. But the tide of a new idea, pushed by the less mature minds in the "movement," flooded the Dani reasoning. Wrangling over bride-prices caused most of the tribal wars and feuds. Therefore, the smooth green stones which they had traded, polished, and caressed through the years were a source of evil and must be destroyed.

At Bokondini on a given day, hundreds crashed their stones into a hole in the ground. One threw away great wealth in three dozen stones and walked away a poor man. Throughout Western Dani, the greater portion of the tribes' currency was buried or burned. Many secretly thought that, with them, they had destroyed the source of sickness and death.

In the maze of devious interpretations of truth half under-

stood, every Dani searched for a way to God. Among the
throng which was rushing from one new thought to the next
and acting upon every breath of rumor, there were those who
were beginning to see that Jesus Christ is the way to God, that
life is a gift from Him through His Son.

To sift the genuine seekers from the bandwagoners, Charles
Horne commenced an "inquirers class" at Bokondini. How to
stop everyone from coming posed a problem. To create a
hardship he set an inconvenient time—eight o'clock on Sunday
morning.

At three o'clock on that morning he heard voices and suspected thieves in the woodshed. Instead, he found several
Mbilu people, from away across the gorge, huddled around a
fire.

"What's the matter? What are you doing here?" he asked.

"Doing? We've come to the meeting. You said to come
early."

By six o'clock the grounds were filled with people and more
were streaming along the airstrip and taxiway. Dismayed,
Horne spoke to the multitude of two or three thousand, the usual Sunday congregation, who had come fearful lest this was
the day for the handing out of eternal life and they would
be losers.

The regular inquirers class attendance finally settled at forty.
These gatherings followed the pattern of the Dani political
and social discussions.

A Dani asked, "Are *deme-deme's* good or bad?" The *deme-
deme* is group courtship, involving chanting and embracing.

"They are not spirit things," another contributed.

"Are they attended only by men looking for a wife?" the
missionary asked.

"Yes."

"Married men go only to get a second wife?"

"Yes."

"Is it good or bad for a child of God to have two wives?"

Out of this followed the consideration of promiscuity and
abortion, age-old practices within their culture.

DANI TWINS. Danis accept twins without superstitious
fear. Babies are carried in string bags suspended from the
mother's forehead. Often a baby will share both bag and
breast with a piglet.

Gradually, these Danis realized the involvement of the Christian life. They began to accept an individual moral reform deeper than a group abandonment of fetishes, fighting, and spirit worship. A sifting began and some were asking, even as they did in our Lord's day, "Who is able for these things?"

The inquiring man refused to accept, unquestioned, the rumors flitting like bats through murky minds.

"The people are saying, 'We must kill our black pigs and breed only white ones, because the black ones make our hearts black.' What does God's word say about that?" they asked.

The missionary put him right about the cause of sin in a man's heart.

Another time came the question, "Tuan Horne, did you really go to Wasua in the airplane? You were away many days and people say, 'He went up to heaven to talk to God like Moses did.' Did you?"

"My friend," answered Horne "You and I can talk with God right here."

"The people are saying, 'Jesus didn't really die. He retained a little life and so revived.'"

The missionary repeated the scriptural account of His death, leaving no doubt of the Lord's decease.

Age-old rituals were not readily set aside for a life of faith. For generations the Danis had anointed their sick with pigs' blood and applied sap of the banana plant to the wound. They had accepted the fact that there was now no more need for the killing of animals because Christ had obtained eternal redemption for them. But they continued to anoint with banana sap, saying, "It is like putting the blood of Jesus on a person to heal him."

"What does the Bible say about that, Tuan?"

"The Bible tells us to use available medicine and pray for the sick."

Until this time the Danis had come together for church services following the only method of assembly that they knew.

Men spent hours arranging their hair into long, mud-coated ringlets, blackening their bodies and adjusting their feathers. Then, massed into prebattle formation, leaping and tossing their curls from side to side, they advanced like an army to the meeting places.

Here, joined by other groups, they ran and danced until their soot-covered bodies glistened with the effort. Then they sat in the open and listened while the witness school men, also plumed and painted, gave their messages. After the manner of their culture, members of the congregation contributed their thoughts on the subject presented.

Although the missionaries had no inclination to ring the people together with a bell from a church belfry, they had grave misgivings as to the worthiness of this weekly spectacle. Yet they hesitated to put an end to it themselves.

While approving indigenous avenues for spiritual expression, caution was needed that they were not unwittingly endeavoring to sanctify evil.

The matter of the loud display of their person as they spoke at the services was discussed with the men of the witness schools.

"We do it so people, especially the women, will look at us," they volunteered.

"Yet you are all married men! Isn't the work of a preacher to witness to Christ, not to draw attention to himself?"

"Men let their hair grow to shake and call the attention of the spirits," the school men added.

"Yet, you say that you have done with spirit things."

The men clipped their hair and washed their bodies. The masses followed. Hundreds, afraid of God and accepting this as another source of merit, cut their hair and washed their bodies.

Some did it deliberately, thoughtfully, weighing the significance of their action.

No-More-Potatoes (Mbyrigwe) sat with his head net off and his long, braided hair resting on his shoulders. The missionary admired it.

No-More-Potatoes turned fiercely, "What's this you say? I let my hair grow to shake at the feasts, to please the spirits. What is this you say about being attractive? It is of the old way—the way I wish to throw out."

Mbyrigwe stood in the midst of his group.

"We have talked about this," he said, "I don't know about you, but I know my mind. I have done with this."

He went off alone and returned with hair short, no head net, and looking miserably cold from his bath in the river.

"I am happy," he said, "I've broken with this thing."

The head net was worn to ensure the goodwill of the spirits. Although some like Blackie from Mulia knew right from the start that he could not have this thing and "follow the Jesus way," many of the older men could not discard the head net. As the "movement" settled down, the older men's acceptance of Christ was evidenced by the removal of his net "skullcap."

With no hair to toss at the spirits and with no bedecked bodies to display to the women, the prechurch dancing gradually ceased. A reverent quietness took its place. As the Danis moved forward in spiritual maturity, their everyday bearing refined, and the expression of their worship developed in such a way that any Christian from any society could have comfortably joined with them.

14

Finding the Substance

THE MISSIONARIES were disturbingly aware that, while reducing social crises emanating from sickness and fear, they were touching only the perimeter of the Dani problem. The center remained untouched. They knew that unless the fundamental need—reconciliation with God—was met, the "movement" would would either abort or give birth to spurious cults, such as "cargo" cultism.

The Danis had been baptized with a moral baptism. They were living in the vacuum made by throwing everything out without receiving any transforming power into their lives. They rushed frantically from one moral reform to another in an effort to satisfy their soul hunger.

Dave Scovill told his people, "You Danis are like a house which you have cleaned. You have tossed out all the rubbish, swept it, washed it, and boarded it up. It is left empty. One day a pig gets in, roots around, and filthies it. Then what is that house like? We need someone to live in there to keep it clean for us. Who? Jesus Christ, the Son of God."

Although teaching on the Holy Spirit had not been neglected, indecision about terminology made presentation difficult. The Danis knew no good spirit and therefore had no word for it. One word expressed the spirit of the dead, another malicious spirits, while yet another the shadow or image. There was no adequate coverage for the Holy Spirit.

The missionaries began to preach the power and work of the Holy Spirit, in the belief that discussions with the Danis following teaching on the subject would bring to light the right word or expression. In time they did find an expression which conveyed the meaning they wished to communicate. To the Danis even this great doctrine of the Holy Spirit became another bandwagon to be boarded. But the discerning missionary could see the pattern which God was weaving, taking shape, as well as the devil's age-old tactics.

Although modern thought calls Satan by psychological names and attributes his wiles to misfunctions of the human mind, his existence is not nullified. No one can overcome his temptations unless they recognize the personality with whom they are dealing. The Stone Age Danis, untroubled by a fashionable approach to an age-old problem, have no doubt that there is a personal devil, the "general director" of the evil spirits that they know so well.

At Kelila in the pewter greyness of an early morning, before the station roused, a young lad, Wolowak-Mbuluk, came to Bert Power with a long string of cowrie shells.

"Tuan, I want to pay for the house I burned down."

"Which house?"

"That empty mission house that burned down months ago. I sneaked in there one night, lit a fire, and fell asleep. While I slept, the house caught on fire. I was afraid and ran away. All this time I have told no one. You have not known who did it. Well, it was I, Wolowak-Mbuluk."

"It was you, was it? I thought it was done by some old women cooking potatoes nearby."

"Yes, I know. I wanted you to think that. But, last night I could not sleep. I sat and talked about God's talk. I saw a great light and knew that it was God talking to me. I cried because of my sin, all my sins. Now I am happy because God's Spirit has come into my heart. For that reason I want to pay for the house."

Seeing this as a genuine conversion, the missionaries rejoiced that here at least was one who had personal dealings with God. In all sincerity they encouraged Wolowak-Mbuluk to tell his experience that others might be helped. However, when a growing exuberance and an unbalanced concentration on prayer and singing accompanied his testimony, it became evident that, whether his initial experience had been genuine or not, he was now being deceived by a counterfeit spirit.

Word of Wolowak-Mbuluk's experience spread through the valleys.

"This is the thing. Be like Wolowak-Mbuluk—cry about your sins and see a great light. That's the way to get the Holy Spirit."

No doubt the story of Paul's conversion strengthened this attitude. All through the villages the people were crying for their sins to try to get this experience. The masses were without true repentance.

Each off-center focal point—moral reform, sorrow over sins, literacy, knowledge of the Scriptures, personal experience—was in itself good. But excessive concentration on each kept their minds from the cross where the redemptive work of Christ was completed and where they had to come before they could begin to receive eternal life.

Mbatlimbulukwe rushed towards Charles Horne and threw her arms around him, crying "Tuan, I've seen the light! I have the Holy Spirit! You're Jesus. You're Jesus!"

"Puk! Be quiet!" he demanded. "You have nothing of the sort. The Holy Spirit does not put lies into a person's mouth. He does not cause people to behave in an unseemingly exaggerated manner. He teaches only the truth about Jesus Christ."

Later Mbatlimbulukwe came to say, "Satan deceived me."

Down in Tenggen Ambut, Pipingawi—with his name changed to *Jetu Amoluk* (Jesus' Spirit)—was acting as number one espionage agent for Satan. He operated on the outskirts of Mulia and Ilu with an accomplice who called himself "Holy Spirit." They mixed truth with untruth.

Under their leadership a group would gather together and sing "*Wa Jetu*" (Welcome Jesus).

While the group sang, a tingling sensation came into their feet, worked up through the body and into the heart, accompanied with a great surge of happiness. Then as Pipingawi chanted over them, "You die. You die," they fell into a type of hypnotic sleep. Again Pipingawi incanted a blasphemous "prayer" in the name of Christ, that they would take hold of life. As they came out of the trance, they were filled with excessive exuberance. They were now supposedly "born again" and had received a new heart. Actually, they had been deceived into looking for concrete evidence instead of acting by faith in God's truth.

This was not a new medium of evil. The missionaries had seen the same rite performed at Sengge when a divining spirit had entered a Papuan to prophesy. It was now being used as an instrument for the greatest possible deception— a counterpart of God's most holy work—the coming of the Holy Spirit to consummate the new birth of a believer into Jesus Christ.

Even some of the genuine were deluded. One of the outstanding women from Mulia submitted herself to this experience. When it was explained to her that this was only a counterfeit, she cried bitterly, "I was so hungry to have everything. How Satan has deceived me!"

Along with this pseudomovement, an authentic work of God was developing. Many in the station Bible schools, which had grown out of the witness schools, had experienced sound new birth in Christ. This had been a quiet, unostentatious experience with some scarcely knowing exactly when it had taken place.

Some said, "When I burned my fetishes I thought I had eternal life. I thought that I had to do all these things to get God's life, but it was Satan's deception. Now I know that Jesus died and rose and gave me life."

Such men had a real spirit of discernment and led their people with wisdom. Sometimes at their meetings, one with much crying would get up and say, "I've seen the light. I've got the Holy Spirit and want to tell the people about it."

A Bible school man would reply with authority, "My friend, sit down. What you have is not the Holy Spirit but an evil spirit."

When Bible school men visited remote areas, desperately sick folk were frequently brought to them. As they prayed over them, some were miraculously healed, and evil spirits were exorcised. The Lord gave these people "signs and wonders."

But with the entering of a counterfeit spirit there were false "signs following." The experience seekers took hold of the genuine and tried to imitate it, until the real was confused with the fake. Some forced their way into the hospital and removed patients in order to pray over them.

The believers were warned from the Word of God not to rejoice that spirits were subjected to them but rather that their names were written in heaven. The missionaries prayed that God would keep His hand on the people and produce sound minds and disciplined lives for the Dani church.

Many were concerned about their sin. Tight control prevented confession of long lists of sins in public places. However, some felt the pressure of the past and the need to unburden to someone.

One night Mbundaga came to the missionary's door.

"My insides are all twisted about because of my sins," he said. "I want to tell you about them."

He had three little bundles of twigs. Undoing one, he placed a twig on the floor.

"This one. I killed a man. When I did that, I crucified Christ."

He had divided his sins into three categories: those permissible in his culture but against the laws of God, those against the group, and immoral trespassing.

When he was finished, the missionary asked, "Where are your sins now, Mbundaga?"

His face lighted up from within. "Jesus has taken them all away," he said.

"Then they can't twist you up any more. Now, forget those things which are past and go forward in a new life with Christ."

The people learned to take their sin to the "only true mediator between God and man—the man Christ Jesus." They accepted the fact that on the cross of Calvary their sins had been dealt with and that God would remember them no more.

Mulikwarek, another night caller, said, "I've come like Nicodemus. When others spoke of Christ dying for them I did not know what they were talking about. But now I know and have come to tell you. I want you to write my name with those who will be baptized."

Thousands of confessed "converts" could have been baptized immediately following the fetish burnings. This could have resulted only in many falling away. A solid church grounded in knowledge of the Scriptures was the objective of the mission. Therefore, with so much counterfeit mingled with the genuine, no one was baptized until his life evidenced that he both understood and acted upon the principles of the Christian faith.

Out of the thousands turning to Christ, only eight Danis were baptized at Kelila on Sunday, July 29, 1962. Four thousand crowded around the pool, among them a group from Bokondini,

BAPTISMAL SERVICE. Four thousand Danis gather for a baptismal service conducted by a national pastor.

their former enemies. No spears. No arrows. Here and there grease, soot, and feathers of those who had come to watch but not yet to participate. No noisy, excited racket of the premovement Danis. Each man and woman was quiet, expectant, reverent.

A little man, Jawon, the first of the candidates, came forward.

"I used to be in great darkness and did many sins. Then I heard the Word of God, and how the Son of God gave His life for me. I believe the Word of God and I am His child. I now confess openly before you all that I am identified with the Lord Who died for me and rose again."

The missionary reached out and took his hand.

"Jawon, do you believe in Jesus Christ the Son of God?"

"*Epe aret* [that is true]."

Then Jawon, the first Kelila Dani, went down into the waters of baptism. One after another, five men and a married couple followed Jawon.

Monthly a steady number was added to the first eight. The Bible school men and their wives were the first baptized in each area. These men, with the missionary acting as adviser, became the first church council. The apostle Paul in forming new churches, advised against the appointment of novices to positions of responsibility. In these early days the nationals and missionaries were much dependent upon each other: the Papuans upon the missionaries' knowledge and experience, and the missionaries upon the Papuans' understanding of their own culture and their personal acquaintance of individual candidates for baptism.

If recommended by the Dani leaders, a candidate went into an Inquirers' Class where he was given a thorough coverage of cardinal doctrines. At the conclusion of the school he was scrutinized by the church council with questions such as these:

> Who is God?
> Is Jesus equal with God?
> Who is Satan? Was he created or in existence eternally?

How did sin come into the world?
What are the results of sin?
Why did Jesus come into the world?
Why did He die?
By what power did He rise again?
Will Jesus come again?
Do you know Jesus as your Saviour?
What is baptism?
Can the old nature go to heaven?
Can the new nature sin?
How can we stimulate growth of the new nature?
If we have new life in Christ, will our bodies die?
Is the gospel the white man's invention?
Are Europeans and Papuans all members of one church?

With their will to learn and receptive minds, even the older men and women intelligently answered such questions.

When Tipon, a married man, came before the council, one of the Dani leaders questioned him, "There's a story abroad about you and a woman. Is this true or not?"

Tipon admitted it. Although the girl had tried to seduce him, he said, "I have sinned in my heart."

Tipon had advanced out of the Dani tendency to excuse one's sins and disown responsibility. Through the presence of the Holy Spirit he had become sensitive to sin. Although he was a man born into an adulterous community, he recognized the teaching of Christ, "If a man looks on a woman with a lustful eye, he has already committed adultery with her in his heart."

Because of the background of the people, the testimony of fellow Christians, and his voluntary admission of lust in his heart, and the need for establishing a church with no weak attitude towards immorality, he was deferred to a future date. God is more concerned with purity for His church than with numbers. Yet, despite the unpopularity of holiness, hundreds were added to the church.

Out of the great mass movement, individuals had come to

make a personal accounting with God. In each area forty to fifty were baptized each month. After each baptismal service Stone Age Dani and the missionary from his sophisticated culture sat together on the floor around the simple Feast of Remembrance prepared of Dani staple food—roast sweet potato —and berry juice, served in a wooden dish and bamboo cups. Reduced to a common level? No. Raised to the highest state man can know—one in Christ Jesus.

A presiding Dani pastor repeated in his own tongue, "For as often as you eat this bread, and drink this cup, you do show the Lord's death till He come."

He broke the potato.

"This is my body which is given for you: this do in remembrance of me."

Together they ate.

He passed the cup.

"This cup is the new testament in my blood: this do you, as often as you drink it, in remembrance of me."

Together they drank.

The wall which had separated them from Christ was broken down by God's love for sinners. Barriers between enemies had been abolished by that same love let loose in the hearts of men.

The Danis had become part of the body of Christ. They had found eternal life.

15

Standing by the Wolos

"WE CAN'T RECEIVE this talk about eternal life. If it had started right here in the Grand Valley, where our tribe came up out of the ground we would listen to it. But because it has come from the fringe it can be of no consequence," said Ukumheatuk, the most powerful of all the Baliem Valley chiefs. This sentiment caught the minds of the proud Central Danis and spread through the tribe, steeling their hearts against the message of life. The Wolos, members of the Central Danis, accepted this attitude too.

During 1961, however, the Wolo missionaries, Bonds and Turners, saw a gradual increase in the church. Earnest men and women one by one weighed tribe against Christ, and in the face of tribal resistance, joined themselves to the first Christians, Emelugun, Arikatdlek, Tamene and his wives.

A dozen in the inquirers class learned from the first draft of a translation of Mark's Gospel. A two-class day school catered for forty-eight pupils. Literacy and Bible classes for adults and a daily medical clinic were available to all.

Tamene and Emelugun took part in ministering in the Sunday services which were attended by about fifty worshippers. Because of medical help given during an epidemic, attendance leaped to five hundred. But opposition from leaders soon brought about a general withdrawal, and the numbers dwindled to the few constant members. The same pressure from the leaders caused the medical work too to fall away. The Wolos wanted to sell a few vegetables to the missionaries but had a general disinterest in their activities.

"If you get rid of your fathers [spirit fetishes] we will get

164

rid of ours," the old men told the missionaries indicating their radios, tape recorders, and cameras.

Although disinterested, the people continued to be friendly towards the missionaries who felt that despite a general lack of enthusiasm the situation was good for the healthy development of a virile church. Because of the pressure upon them, the people were forced to consider the cost before they joined the Christians. Thus only those who were sincere in their dealings with God came into the church fellowship.

Concurrently with the Wolo decline in interest in Christian teaching, a crisis had been developing between them and the Ilugwa groups. For years feuds between the Wolos and Baliems, at the mouth of the Wolo River, had fostered bitter enmity. Allied, the Wolo and Ilugwa tribes had kept their Baliem enemies in their place. Although jointly confederated with some Wolos resident in the Ilugwa Valley, the situation between the two groups was often tense.

During this time an important Ilugwa man visited his relatives down in the Wolo basin. While he was there, another

LITERACY CLASS. A literacy class among the Danis perseveres.

Ilugwa, also visiting in the same section, became ill and died. The surviving visitor was blamed and assassinated. Relationships between the Ilugwas and Wolos immediately deteriorated.

The Baliem Danis, seeing their old enemies with a weakened alliance, began to harry them. Wolo Chief Bidi went to Pass Valley, where the American C-47 had crashed, to ask old friends to come back to Wolo. He had gone without consulting his Ilugwa relatives, who not so long ago had helped him to push back the Pass Valley people. As a result tensions tightened and snapped into sporadic fighting between the Ilugwas and Wolos.

Reinforcements from Pass Valley poured into Wolo. The great pile of Wolo and Pass Valley spears stacked for pre-battle dedication as well as their numerically superior strength failed to lift Chief Bidi's spirits. Nothing could move the Wolo conviction that the Ilugwas would wipe them out.

The Ilugwas allied themselves with their former hated enemies from the Baliem. This forced the Wolos into the center of a pincer movement.

In March, 1962, the Baliems pushed up from the southwest; the Ilugwas came in from the east and squeezed the Wolos out of the top end of the valley. They burned twenty-five villages and butchered the fleeing refugees. Their arrows perforated a helpless old man. They stabbed a child on the back of a fleeing mother. They caught a girl and hurled her over a cliff on to the rocks below. The Baliems were paying back the Wolos for years of savagery.

The Wolos fought with every skill and weapon. But, as the Ilugwas and Baliems pushed them back they became completely demoralized. They believed they had lost their *amulok kuniks*. The spirits were no longer with them. Defeat was already in their hearts.

The pro-Christian Wolos had said to Russell Bond, "When the Ilugwas come, we'll bring our pigs and come down and live on the mission station."

"You can come," replied Bond, "but I have no weapons, no warriors. I cannot protect you."

But they were determined to shelter on the mission station, believing that its very precincts would give supernatural protection.

Labittiwe, whose son helped in the Bond kitchen, told them, "When you see that village on the ridge burning, you send my son to me and we'll bring my pigs down into the mission yard."

At midday the village burned. The boy went to his father and returned with him bringing the pigs.

House after house belched smoke and blazed into searing flames as victory-maddened Ilugwas rushed through the villages with burning faggots and flaying axes. Terrified Wolos, carrying what they could, streamed from the inferno. They drove their pigs before them, dragged them on their leads, or slung them onto their shoulders. A hundred homes burned behind three thousand fleeing refugees. The aged, the lame, and infirm could not leave. Those who tried were caught and slaughtered. Two hundred Wolo Danis jammed onto the mission station. The others, spurning the mission, fled over the hills to relatives in Jugumbaga and the Tagi Valley. The yelling Ilugwas, burning and killing, advanced on the mission station.

Russell Bond called through the radio to MAF pilot, Bob Johansen, who flew to Bokondini and picked up police and the government officer, Huisingha, who had been kept informed of the Wolo trouble. As the Cessna came in to land at Wolo through thick smoke, heavy with the smell of burning flesh, the Ilugwas had reached a grassy knoll a mile from the station, where the Wolo warriors were making a desperate stand.

Huisinga tried to parley with the Ilugwas but they yelled, "Go home! Go on! Go back to your house." He replied by firing over their heads. The volley from the police guns decided the Ilugwas against further advance.

A peace, through a promised pig payment, brought temporary abatement. People trickled back and occupied the undamaged houses in the Wolo basin. A thousand less fortunate lived in hovels, pig shelters, and under bushes until they could rebuild. A hundred refugees slept on mission verandas, under houses, and even in chicken and goat houses. Lil Bond, who with her children had been evacuated to Bokondini, returned to Wolo and treated those ill with influenza, which had spread through the groups, further depressing the mentally defeated Wolos.

Their Pass Valley confederates, fearing annihilation in an alliance with a people who had lost the power of the spirits, pulled out and returned to their own country.

The Jugumbagas, to whom the Wolos had fled, treated them as spirit-despised and conquered. They stole their pigs and molested their women. Alone, the men could have sneaked back to Wolo at night. But, with their women, children, and pigs they could not leave without oppression. In their fear and demoralized condition, produced by the loss of their *amulok kunik*, they had lost the will to make a way to escape.

Tamene, Emelugun, and two other Christians, not being dependent on the spirits, had not lost their courage. Dressed in their best and unarmed, they strode into the Jugumbaga group.

"Get your stuff," they ordered the refugees, "and come on."

The Jugumbagas sat still and watched the now emboldened Wolos collect their belongings, their women, and children and follow the four men who had come for them.

Mbidi, Titlok, and other big chiefs, who had persecuted the Christians, were among those who were rescued. Now, with shame, they brought pay, which was refused, to these young men for delivering them and all their possessions, without loss, out of the hands of thieving "friends."

Threats and forays from the Baliem preserved the tension and increased the fears of the people. The cat scratching on a door in the night was enough to cause the Bonds to spring from their beds.

Refugees moving back from Tagi or Pass Valley were shot at and sometimes killed. Many returned to their own borders under the cover of night.

The bulk of the Dutch constabulary was primarily occupied

with Indonesian infiltration along the south and western coasts, so that only a minimum of police could be placed at Wolo. The people were afraid to go to distant gardens to harvest crops without a police guard. Produce in remaining gardens was soon used up and new gardens were not made. Hunger now added to their problems.

With the payment of peace pigs between the groups, the police withdrew and life returned to a degree of normality within a tight circuit of the mission station. New houses were built against the compound, but the people still feared to harvest distant gardens and limited new garden areas did not solve their food problems.

Within the outer circle of tension and intrigue, the missionaries continued a restricted ministry. Showing an inner serenity, the Christians encouraged each other and helped the returning refugees to rebuild their homes.

When the situation looked as though it might even out, the Ilugwas attacked suddenly and viciously. A group of Wolos going for firewood was cut down ten minutes from the mission house.

With the newly built Wolo houses huddled now closer together around the station, there was no warning before the enemy was already in their midst, killing and burning. When the enemy again attacked, refugees crowded on to the mission compound. Russell Bond called again through the radio. The MAF pilot flying to the Wamena base heard his call, picked up a police patrol from the government post at Wamena, and turned back to Wolo. At Wolo the missionaries waited, searched the sky for a speck moving towards them, listened for the sound of an engine bringing relief, prayed that the little yellow plane would race the advancing horde now within minutes of the station.

Crazed with sure victory, the Ilugwas massed on the grassy ridge behind the compound in a final dance to terrorize the miserable Wolos, already as good as dead by their reckoning. Feathered and triumphant, they threw themselves into ecstatic abandonment, displaying their prowess, shouting threats and insults, gloating over the victims about to be slaughtered.

Inside the compound, looking down on the dancing horde, the two missionaries stood with the Wolo Christians gathered around them. They encouraged each other, confident in their God for whatever they may have to face. They knew that minutes after the leader gave the signal, the merciless, butchering horde would be upon them. Panic was suppressed and they did not react with cries of terror as the Ilugwas had expected. Neither did they break and run in a bid for safety to make sport for their enemies. So the Ilugwas, somewhat nonplussed, danced some more and shouted louder threats.

The pilot brought the Cessna in, roared low, skimming the heads of the attackers, scattering some and pushing others to the ground, throwing all into confusion. As the aircraft came to a halt, the police jumped out, machine guns at the ready. The attack was repelled.

Everyone knew that it was only a temporary respite. The Ilugwas threatened, "Next time we will come in the night. Then your planes and radio will not save you."

"The big hand of God has kept us safe," said Tamene. He knew that if the Ilugwas had not paused to boast, help would have come too late. The missionaries knew, too, that thousands of steamed-up Danis could put an end to three or four police, machine guns and all, if they put their mind to it.

Charles Horne called upon the Dutch Highland District Commissioner, whose natural inclination was to control the inland, but because of outside political pressure could promise only deterioration in police protection.

Two days later, Horne flew into Wolo to discuss its future with Russell Bond and Wal Turner, who had recently returned from furlough. To keep the Wolo personnel to numbers which could be evacuated in one flight, Nan Turner and the children had been diverted to Kelila instead of returning to Wolo after their furlough in Australia. Now, it had to be decided whether it would be right to keep on occupying the station.

Apart from those herded into the hundred or so houses

around the airstrip and a handful of people in a distant valley, the Wolo basin was empty. Those around the mission had come there because they looked to the mission radio and MAF airplanes to bring police aid. Police protection could no longer be guaranteed. With the houses so close, there would be no time, in a sneak attack, for even limited help to reach them. It was obvious that without miraculous intervention, the missionaries would be slaughtered with those whom they sheltered.

The Wolos were hungry, afraid to garden, and demoralized.

After five years of travail, the missionaries were loath to surrender this station. In recommending evacuation Charles Horne said, "Up to one thousand people are staking their lives on our radio and plane. Even if we can get a message out we cannot depend on police aid coming in. The political situation is such that the district commissioner could promise nothing after the end of the month. By staying we are deluding the people. But when we go, we must take those who want to come with us."

On September 29 and 30 the Cessna flew load after load of equipment and material out of Wolo, until everything worth the air freight had been dismantled and removed. Under police escort the people began to move. A long trail, laden with their belongings, moved up over the pass and down into areas where fighting and hate had turned to peace and compassion.

Turning away from the land of his fathers, Tamane said, "These houses of wood and grass are not our true homes. They will rot and burn. Our true homes are in heaven and no one can take them from us."

Both Bokondini and Wolo Christians had said, "The Wolos can live with us."

Those who gave thought to the Christian way joined the Wolo believers and inquirers, bringing the total to two hundred. Confident of a Christian welcome, they braved a situation where formerly they would have been robbed and killed, and shared their hosts' houses and food until they could provide for themselves.

There were those on the fringe of the Kelila community who tried to exploit the misplaced Wolos by abusing their women and treating them as inferior beings who had lost their *amulok kunik*. Big Malok slapped one smart alecky fellow on his bare buttocks with a flat board and shook him like a terrier with a rat.

"Now mind your ways," he said. "We are not as those with no strength who have fled before their enemies. At no time did the Ilugwas drive us out of our country. God stood by us and we left of our own free will, for no other reason than that we came here to learn God's Word in peace."

Although he had moved into the airstrip for protection old chieftain Mbidi refused to leave Wolo.

"I will not go. I will die and rot here," he announced.

A few stayed with him.

After the evacuation there was no more fighting and most of the evacuees to the Tagi and Pass Valley moved back. They burned the mission houses for the nails and planted gardens on the site. Fortunately, they preserved the airstrip.

At first, the displaced Wolo Danis were shy and bewildered, depending much on their missionaries, the Turners at Kelila, and the Bonds at Bokondini. Gradually they merged with the locals, joining the literacy and school classes. Emelugun and Tamene took their places with the local leaders. In the disruption of normal life, tribal pressures eased and Emelugun married the Christian girl he wanted in a simple ceremony free from spirit rites.

When both Bonds and Turners, through ill health were forced to leave West New Guinea, the displaced Wolos were bereft of their ministry. But this threw them more upon local leadership and helped to integrate them into their adopted churches.

Crises in the church should always result in triumph and growth. Although the circumstances may appear to be a complete rout by the enemy, if the participants are Christ-centered, victory and progress must emerge.

16

Your Father-in-law's Name

AN "AMEN" rumbled through the great crowd at the close of the last prayer.

An Indonesian veterinary surgeon, posted by the new government to Hollandia, now Djaya Pura, had come to Bokondini to check the mission cattle. He stayed on overnight so that he could attend the early morning church service. As the "amen" ebbed to silence, he turned, deeply moved, to the missionary in charge.

"You people are not concerned with politics, but with the souls of men," he said.

Although following a different faith, he saw that the political upheavals stirring the country did not alter the missionary objective. These men were simply ambassadors for Christ. They had been sent by God to preach a gospel which brought life to every man no matter what his political involvement.

Eight hundred to a thousand people: white-haired men leaning on their sticks, mothers with babies on their backs, bright-eyed girls, and clean-limbed youths walked for an hour or more each morning, down hills, over ridges, and through gorges to attend the eight o'clock Bible class.

Gone was their noisy exuberance and excited agitation of fighting days, when they used to behave like a disturbed football crowd. Now they sat quietly reverent, absorbing Christian doctrines and ethics. What they learned they applied to their own situation.

Breathing out a tremulous sigh of appreciation and anticipation for a better way of life, the people rose at the end of the

173

Family Reading. A family shares in reading from crude
primers.

morning's lesson, and quietly returned to their hamlets and
gardens. There had been a time when they had stayed on all
day praying in groups, learning stories, or spelling out the new
words of a primer.

"You must go back to your homes and dig your gardens, tend
your pigs, and build your fences. Christ is within you, not just
here where you listen to the preaching. We must live as well
as learn," the missionaries told the new converts.

After this, only those in the literacy classes remained at the
station for an extra hour so so. Hundreds around every mission station were learning to read. Those who mastered the
art taught others.

At Bokondini as soon as a man or woman had learned ten
lessons, he collected charts, flash cards, and primers from the
mission and taught a group of ten, while he himself kept a few
paces ahead in a more advanced grade. As the number of
classes increased, all available classroom space in existing buildings, including outhouses and laundries, was taken up. The
readers then built themselves grass shelters where they could
have lessons protected from sun or rain. As the work grew and

trained pastors went into outlying areas, the literacy campaign was decentralized too, with teachers spreading out into these areas.

Over at Ilu Dave Cole held a flashcard before his Bible school literacy class. On it was printed *tewe,* the generic word for bird. Many New Guineans take their names from birds, trees, flowers, or other objects around them. Cole held up the card and waited for Ap-enuk to read it.

The fellow looked at it and hesitated. Then with a rush said, *penarek,* the particular name of a specific bird.

"Oh, come," said Dave, "You know this word."

A classmate whispered, "That word on the card is also the name of his father-in-law. He cannot say it."

The men relaxed, thinking, *Now that Cole knows that the word is the name of his wife's father, he will pass over it.*

But Cole looked at them.

"You fellows say that you are following Jesus, but you are still tied up with deception. You think that sickness will come to you if you say your father-in-law's name."

Ap-enuk was embarrassed. It was true what the Tuan had said. The sympathetic but apprehensive stares of his fellow students did not ease his discomfort. Then, his face lightened with a streak of cunning.

"Well, what's your father-in-law's name, Tuan? You say it."

An impish grin teased Cole's face.

"*My* father-in-law's name?" he said with simulated concern.

"Yes, your father-in-law. You say his name."

"The name of my wife's father is Reimeyer."

"What? Say it again!"

Cole said it again.

"I am the child of God. The *kuki* [chief spirit] cannot touch me while I'm in Him. Satan has lied to you and you have listened. Saying people's names cannot hurt you and it cannot harm them."

Cole turned to one of the keenest in the group and asked, "What is the name of your wife's father?"

The fellow sat quietly thinking. Then, squaring his shoulders,

176 AN HOUR TO THE STONE AGE

said emphatically, "The name of my father-in-law is Apinak."

There was a stunned silence. A man had deliberately challenged the *kuki*.

Their relief to be free of that bit of bondage was so great that once out of school, they grabbed the first man they saw. Lacking the enlightenment that the students had just experienced, the poor fellow took fright and, thinking that these Bible school men were trying to victimize him, fled to the hills. As time passed, however, with the deception in that department uncovered, the men began freely to use the name of their paternal in-law.

At this time, the literacy program at Mulia was showing remarkable results. Leon Dillinger and Dave Scovill had prepared a set of progressive primers which took the readers through to fluency. These were distributed to the hundreds who wanted to learn to read. At one time there were 750 on the roll. A starter attached himself to a literate.

"Tell me again what this says. I've forgotten."

"*Ke-nu.*"

He would repeat the word over and over until he had equated sight and sound.

Twice a week Scovill and Dillinger tested scores of readers before graduating them to the next primer. Hundreds of retarded Mulias learned to read with fluency, despite the warnings of medical men that the mission could not expect to run a normal school in the district of cretins.

Without doubt, medication and missionary teaching had changed the course of Mulia history. They were new creatures with new interests, new occupations, and with a zest to progress in this new life. Warring had turned to learning, *kuki* worshipping to God praising, blood sacrificing to heart-cleansing, and fearing to trusting.

With the drive for knowledge pounding through the valleys, the missionaries told the Mulias, "We shall build a large school so that we can teach you more than just reading. Those who already know how to read and do numbers will teach those who don't. We shall tell you about other countries and other subjects, as well as more about the Bible. But first we shall need wood and workers to build this school."

All the next week axes bit into the hillside timber. Happy people called to each other and sang. At the end of a week, enough wood to erect one building 100 feet by 30 feet and another 90 feet by 40 feet had been brought in. Dave Scovill paced a log 55 feet long by 14 inches at the base and 8 inches at the tip. Twenty-five men had carried it to the building site.

Their skills in group activity and their proficiency in organization had brought quick results in the log felling. Each man as a member of a team knew what he was to do and did it.

On the appointed morning for the thatching of the school, thousands came with *kunai* grass which they had cut and tied into appropriate bundles. Certain men climbed the rafters, caught and tied the bundles thrown to them by men designated to this job. The rest kept up the supply of grass. In three hours, the 40 by 90-foot building had been thickly thatched.

The Dani organizing ability is also evident in their tribal feastings. At a feast where three thousand had gathered, pit ovens were prepared, food assembled, cooked, and evenly distributed in half a day. Each team member was whipped into activity by enthusiastic leadership. Europeans present tried to calculate what time and effort would be put into preparing for an equivalent number at an outdoor church picnic in Western civilization.

The Danis are a highly intelligent people. They have been retarded from developing according to present-day standards of civilization only through lack of opportunity. An American psychiatrist, Dr. Henry Brandt, estimated that given this opportunity, these gifted organizers could take their place in contemporary culture in less than twenty years.

The tremendous Dani energy previously expended in warring and spirit feasting had to be channeled into effective projects. No-man's-lands were turned into productive gardens, with a corresponding improvement in the health of the people. Fewer rust-colored heads, due to vitamin deficiency, dotted the crowds. Tension symptoms became less noticeable.

Dani culture majors on feasting. With the coming of the gospel, spirit-feasts turned to Happiness Feasts, held at working parties, marriages, conventions, or for the sheer delight of celebrating their new happiness.

Christian conventions running for a few days were held in central areas. People from neighboring tribes came for fellowship and teaching. Old scout-guarded wartrails became highways to friendship.

The Roman Caesars had built roads for pacification. The Mulia missionaries had only to mention this to their people, and the Danis were away on an enthusiastic road-building program. The Ilu Danis too took up the project. Starting from their respective stations, they joined land which had been trampled by frenzied war feet and wet with warrior blood. On their behalf the missionaries approached the government and received wheelbarrows, shovels, crowbars, and picks. There were not enough to go around the hundreds of workers. Many used digging sticks, bags for barrows and their bare hands to shovel dirt.

An old chief took upon himself the oversight of the road construction saying, "I can't learn in school, but I can do my part."

Under his leadership, the Mulias slashed down rain forests, dug out hillsides, bridged plunging mountain streams, and filled swamps and rain-washed ravines with hand-carried rocks. They zig-zagged up a razorback, sliced off the top of a ridge, and laid the road along it before carving out the hillside into the next valley. Owners moved houses and uprooted gardens to give the road unhindered progress. When a thirty-foot boulder blocked the way, the "civil engineers" would allow no deviating bend. They lit fires around the rock to split it and bit by bit chipped it away.

Then the old overseer became very ill, and realizing that the end of his life was near, he gave instructions for the completion of the road. When he died, his men worked on to complete the highway.

The fifteen-foot, well-graded gravel road smooths the eight-

·een rugged miles from Mulia to Ilu and being commonly owned has given freedom to those who were once enemies to pass through the others' territory as well as enabling distant groups to come to the mission station more frequently. The missionaries, given this easy motorcycle access, could sustain a ministry down in the Yambo, the birthplace of so many heresies.

The Danis took to improving their homes and gardens. A woman with a bundle of seed grass on her head explained to Stan Sadlier, "I am going to make my garden beautiful, too. From our village up on the hill, we look down and see yours, beautiful with grass and flowers where once it was nothing but mud. Ours too will be beautiful."

The people built their own churches, great thatched roofs with open sides to allow for the regular overflow of congregation. They leveled off the ground and planted grass and flowers around them. Where once there had been ugliness and dirt, now there was a pride in the beauty and neatness of their surroundings.

Commencing with marriage, the Dani society was being established on Christian principles. Jabingga, a leader from Kelila, stood at the conclusion of his daughter's wedding and said, "We are thankful to God for the tremendous changes which the gospel has brought to our people. We have taken the evil out of our wedding ceremonies. In future, all our Christian weddings will be as this first one here at Kelila. In the church the men and women will make their promises to God and to each other to be true people."

While teaching Christian ethics from Holy Scripture, the missionaries made no move to change the customs of the Danis. Any innovations in their culture came spontaneously from themselves. The missionaries had come to lay before the Danis the terms of God's kingdom. They had come to promote the supremacy of God. In accepting Christian precepts, the Dani relationship to the kingdom could result only in blessing to themselves and others instead of misery and hatred.

17

No Longer Big Men

POMBI, A MULIA MAN, had helped the missionaries build their houses. Then he took a wife from among the down-valley people whom the Mulias had pushed over the cliff and driven out of their land. Dave Scovill gave Pombi an ax to cut bamboo for building the new home.

Pombi went down to his wife's valley by a back way, planning to cut the bamboo and return with his wife. She was visiting her people, who were now drifting back into their former territory. He did not expect to meet with any trouble because he had good acceptance with his wife's relations.

Made welcome, he joined a group around a fire. With his head bowed over his knees, he let his hair fall over his face while friends searched it, cracked lice, and sucked them noisily into their eager mouths. His ax lay at his side.

A down-valley chief approached the group, picked up Pombi's ax, and slashed his head open.

When news of the slaying reached Mulia, everyone looked at Waritmban to see how he would avenge his brother's death. He was a big man in his village and not given to passing by an insult. As he had been among the first to be baptized, the people waited to see what his reaction in this crisis would be.

The following Sunday, Waritmban stood up at the service and said, "You people are expecting me to avenge my brother. That is not our way in Christ. We have forgiven."

The villagers took their cue from Waritmban, and decided to take no action against their old enemies. Such a killing cannot be considered as an individual murder as it would be in a Western culture. It was a sneer and a challenge to the

180

whole tribe who had effected a victory over a people who would not accept a position of defeat. The retaliation would have to be set in motion by the insulted brother. Waritmban, however, chose to turn the other cheek and entered among those named blessed as peacemakers.

After that, from time to time, people with some interrelationship within the two groups moved between Mulia and the down-valley people. Once, when sitting with a group which included a man from this valley, one of the Mulia men said to Dave Scovill, "Tuan, if we were not hearing God's Word, we would kill this man right now."

With only those with ties of kinship moving back and forth, Scovill decided it was time he visited the valley. Waritmban met Dave and his party on the valley path at the top of the airstrip.

"Tuan," he asked, "Shall I come with you or not?"

He knew that although he had not avenged his brother he was still a wanted man, marked for revenge, for his part in the massacre of these people.

"You decide for yourself. You know the risk which you take," Scovill answered.

"I feel in my heart that God wants me to go with you."

He hesitated a moment, then set his jaw. "I will come with you."

So they went together down into the valley.

The first night they slept on the Mulia side of the boundary line. The next day, coming up through gardens towards a village, Waritmban said in a low voice to Scovill, "That's where the man who killed my brother lives. I am afraid."

Steeling himself with courage, he entered the village, but kept toward the center of his companions. Some leading warriors came out of the huts and approached the visitors. Waritmban viewed them, trying to assess their reaction to his presence.

They stopped before the group and pointing to Waritmban demanded, "Tuan, who is this man beside you? We know who he is. He is Waritmban."

"Yes, it is I." Waritmban aswered. "Before I would have come to kill. Now I've come with God's good words. If you want to kill me, here I am."

"No, we're finished with that," the men replied. "That belongs to our past. We are not remembering any of those things. We want God's Word."

When they had talked with these men about God's true way, Scovill and his band moved on. Approaching another village Waritmban moved in close to Dave.

"If they do anything to me, it will be here at this village. If they kill me, will you take my body home?"

"Waritmban," Dave answered, "You don't have to go on. You can leave right now. You know the path—you can go back home."

"No," he said. "I feel in my heart that God is telling me to go on."

When they entered the village, there were no men at home, so they called across the valley to where they could see the men gathering pandanus fruit. In the meantime, the visitors waited for their return. Scovill and Waritmban sat side by side under a tree. They were not talking, just waiting. Dave watched a powerful man climbing towards them and leading the returning villagers. He knew that on this man was laid the responsibility of any revenge killing. He came across and snapped fingers with Scovill. Then dropping to his knees he threw his arms around Waritmban and hugged him. The hate of years ebbed away, and love and brotherhood flowed in. There was no need for words, but strong men, looking on, wiped their eyes with the heel of their hands.

That night the party slept in the headman's house. The next day the chief stood at the meeting and addressed his people.

"Who has come down here to tell us God's Word? There is a missionary at Mulia, a missionary at Ilu, and another at Ilaga, but today these who were our enemies have come to tell us. From today we want God's Word."

After that, those with no kinship connections began to go to Mulia. Now the valley people have moved back to their old site where they lived before the Mulias drove them out. They have planted flowers around their houses and have built a road into the station. Some have come up to the Mulia school and sit together with the men who killed their fathers.

A new tenderness towards the unfortunate had also entered Dani hearts. Kalekale was one who put his hand into the hand of God. Born deaf, he knew the torture of ridicule from sadistic Danis. His ugly efforts at speech evoked laughter from those who could not recognize the alert mind behind the groping tongue. He had learned to lip read and with eyes focused on the preachers, he absorbed Bible truths. Because of the new love in their hearts, his people grew more sympathetic towards him and took time to teach him and to listen to his questions. His stumbling words, "I want to be baptized," were understood only by his friends.

With the rejection of Mongirat, sorceresses went out of business. Oma, the one-time leading magic-maker, has changed her necklaces of charms and pigs' tails for green popbeads, a gift from a doctor who had been researching goiter at Mulia. Instead of leading the dance formations with her feather "duster" waving away the spirits, she looked for baptism. As she was questioned, the Dani leaders said, "Tuan, she's old. She'll never get it straight in her head. Her tongue gets mixed up, but her heart is straight."

"I'm so happy," she told Ralph Maynard. "You're still young, but me, I'm old. I'll get to see Jesus before you do."

While many were accepting the new order, others fought against it. A few men from the far side of Ngguragi to the east of Mulia, where heresies had been born, came up to the mission school. At their request, Dave Scovill went with some Christian men down into their area. On the first day of their visit, they were well accepted by the fringe people and treated to a feast.

The next day while on the trail, Scovill overheard a fellow say, "That's the track that leads down into the bad man's house."

"How far?" he asked.

"Quite close."

"Well, let's go."

Because this village had opposed the fetish burnings and fired arrows at itinerant evangelists, the visitors went cautiously up the trail, watching for signs of hostility. As they entered the village, a man chopping wood greeted them warmly and invited them in. But other men, armed and with long greased hair, watching from a doorway, shouted to them. "We are Satan's sons. We don't want God's Word here."

"Can we snap fingers with you?" asked Dave Scovill, going forward with the knuckle of his forefinger bent in friendly greeting.

But the man scorned it, brushing it aside with a brusque, "No."

"Can we talk with you awhile?"

But they refused that request too.

Knowing that they were rejecting the Son of God and not him, Scovill did not readily give way.

"Look, we'll just sit here for a while. We'll not talk about God's Word if you don't want it," he said.

"No you don't. That's the track," the chief said, pointing with his arrows. "You go."

Scovill hesitated, but his men said, "Come on, Tuan, let's go."

So they turned and went down the track toward another hamlet. As they walked into the compound the village appeared deserted. Doors were boarded up and not even a pig grunted. But the evangelists knew that the people had shut themselves inside their houses.

"Looks as though there is nobody home," said Scovill in a loud voice. "We had better go on to the next hamlet."

Instead, he jumped over a fence and went around to a back door. It was wide open with twenty or so men, including four big chiefs, crowded inside the hut. Dave walked in and sat with them. Surprise stifled their resistance.

"Listen, you fellows," he said. "We have not come to force

God's Word on you. We just want to be your friends. If you
want your old way, that's all right by us."

A loud voice protested from the center of the room, "On your
way—go on, get out. We don't want these words. We haven't
straightened out our hearts yet. Move on."

The evangelists moved on, their hearts heavy that these
Ngguragi people refused to learn about God.

"We'll not go about cramming Bible verses into their ears,"
Scovill told his companions. "We will help them all we can.
When they are in trouble and need help we shall go to them.
We'll help them build their fences and their houses."

Five months later, one of the evangelists said to Dave Scovill, "Tuan, you remember that man who wouldn't let us into
his house? Well, on Sunday he burned his fetishes and weapons."

One by one the whole Ngguragi group did the same.

The gospel had spread into every corner of the western
Dani country. The other Protestant missionary societies were
also experiencing this outreach in their Dani work. To further
the unity of their teaching, not only were conferences held in
an intermission level, but also among Dani Church leaders
from various societies. Again fear and distrust were overridden
as fifty-one Dani leaders hitherto unknown to each other and
representing eleven Dani areas met together at the first of these
conferences which was held on February 12, 1963. The Dani
delegates who had been confined to the limits of their own tribe
were excited by the breadth of the Christian church, the unity
of the believers, and the unanimity of decision after amicable
discussion. In previous palavers a debater had made his point
with the threat of a spear.

In the light of their new standing in Christ, many cultural
matters needed revision. In introducing the problem of bride-
price, a representative from Katubaga declared that they did
not want something "ripped off the old." "It is just as easy to
adopt a new way of marriage as it is to learn new words, and
new ways of living, gardening, and building houses, as we did
after hearing God's Word," they said.

The missionaries were loath to see a complete abolishment of the bride-price and "free brides" brought in, lest it introduce easy divorce. Heavy discussion, however, revealed how burdensome the bride-price had become. Deep-rooted involvements created problems not easily resolved. Finally they appealed to the missionaries for guidance. An earlier Dani suggestion of four pigs paid only to parents and the responsible older brother was adopted for a trial period. There was no thought to revive the use of the spirit stones which they had already buried.

At following Dani conferences, leaders discussed the future place that pigs, associated with old spirit sacrifices, would take in their new culture. The position of the older man, whose power had been weakened, was also considered. In their zeal for the new way, younger school men had unconsciously supplanted the older leaders, adding to the hostility of some against the gospel.

"The names of these old men will remain. They will not be without prestige in gardening, building, feasting, and target shooting," it was agreed.

In a short time some of these older men came to take a place of leadership within the church. Tobaga, who had stood under the trees warily watching the missionaries enter the Bokondini valley back in 1956, was the first of these old patriarchs to be baptized. Where once he had been a general of the army, now he was a leader of the older people, a father to the pastors, and a counselor to the young.

Yunggumulok, a compatriot of Tobaga, had followed behind the fighting group, rounding up the stragglers and spurring on the warriors. Now, crippled by a knee infection following a battle wound, he was carried to the baptismal pond. His friends lifted his stretcher high so that he could speak to the crowd.

"I was like Paul," he said. "Paul bound the Christians and afflicted them. God changed him. I was like that. I have caused suffering and death and God has changed me."

The pastors strained forward, their upturned faces reflecting their joy in what God had done in this old man.

Western Dani was like a giant pot stirred by the Holy Spirit. Each ring rippled out to the next until the whole was agitated. Natural Dani attitude shot out the lip at the neighbor. "Who cares? Let him go to hell. It's good enough for the likes of him." But now each Spirit-moved Christian concerned himself with the well-being of his neighbor.

Knowing that their enabling to live the Christian life and lead the church did not come from the missionaries but from Jesus Christ who was the power within them, more and more Danis were taking responsibility in church leadership. When told that the Hornes were returing to Wasua in the Australian Territory, Pastor Unak, after the first shock of losing a mainstay, answered, "We are not following a man, we are following Jesus Christ. When you go, Jesus will still be here."

Until the graduation of the first local Bible school men, up to one thousand had been coming to the stations daily for in-

struction. Now with national pastors stationed in central villages, they could stay in their own areas and have the pastors minister to them.

"Now my old legs will not have to climb the long mountain trail everyday," said an old man.

With the development of the national church, a central Bible school was commenced with thirty-two students in 1964. As the educational entrance standard of the students improves, the school is gradually being upgraded. Apart from theology, Christian ethics, and homiletics, certain secular subjects, including the Indonesian language, are also being taught.

At Kelila thousands from all neighboring districts gathered for a farewell feast to the first four students leaving from their group to enter the central Bible school in its commencement year. When the steaming pits had been opened and the waiters had distributed the food to the rows of guests, Kipmarek, the Kelila pastor, told his people:

"We are gathered here from every church group in the Kelila district, that we as a unit may know the church council's decision to separate Mandin, Malok, and Mben and their families to enter the central Bible school, to be further trained to take future pastorates among us.

"Let us remind you that we believe they have been chosen of God and sent out at His desire by us, all of us, the church. We must not forget them, but bear the responsibility on their behalf.

"Our people are spreading out far and wide. Let us make sure that here at home our roots are strong in the Lord, that we may lift them up and with them see the Devil defeated and many turn to the Lord and become mature Christians."

Malok, a refugee from Wolo, accepted by the Kelila people as one of their own, was among those being farewelled. In the early days of his conversion he had championed the afflicted and spread the gospel. Soon after his arrival at Kelila, he had joined the preaching parties and gone out to Eragayam, at that time still an enemy group and hostile to the gospel. A mean fellow, the leader of the group, had been stealing pigs from the Christians. When the total rose to ten pigs and one woman, Malok tied him up and marched him in to the police post. His motive had not been age-old payback but relief for the oppressed. Then when the police put the man into the local jail, Malok went in and preached to him. But he remained unrepentant, avowing, "If Malok ever comes through my country I will put an arrow into him."

Free from their leader's oppression during his imprisonment, the Eragayam group burned their fetishes and made full repayment for the pigs that had been stolen. By the latter part of 1965 three churches were opened in this area with a missionary outreach from each one of them.

When faced with perplexing decisions concerning such matters as marriage, discipline, church government, and political responsibilities, again and again the people asked, "What does the Bible say about this matter?" So that they might read the answer for themselves, the translation of Scripture became a high priority in the mission program. At the end of 1965 the gospels of Matthew and Luke, teachings from the epistles to the Corinthians, the book of Daniel and other portions from the Minor Prophets had been translated by David Scovill and Menno Heyblom. By mid-1969, Genesis, the gospel of John, Acts, most of Paul's epistles, Hebrews, and the epistles of John were all circulating among the people in duplicated form.

Hence the church has been strengthened by the Word of God and fellowship in local groups and area conventions. The Danis have not remained local in their outlook, but their prayers have reached out for the church beyond their own borders to include Australia, America, and the islands of the sea. In their delight in being incorporated into this great fellowship, they did not forget their neighbors who were still without Christ. Neither was their interest confined to prayer meetings, but they made themselves personally responsible for the scattered groups further out.

In conference, while considering the needs of these groups, church leaders decided that airstrips should be built in central places; that pastors would evangelize and minister in these

areas as trained men became available; and until such time as
their own leaders were fully trained, missionaries would over-
see the whole work.

When the Danis first burned their fetishes their concept
of God was a distorted image after the pattern of the only
deity they knew. They judged His character to be in the
mold of the demons, someone who must be appeased before
they could receive a benefit. Now by revelation they knew a
holy and righteous God who gave because it was His nature
to love. This brought them into the eternal life they had long
awaited.

Eternal life, their *Nepalan Kepalan,* came not through the
knowledge of a Christian way of life but through knowing
Christ Himself. With that knowledge has come a transforma-
tion, a change of values, a new assessment of life.

A proud, much decorated chief, whose consuming desire
had been to be a "big man," voiced their acknowledged acceptance of the sovereignty of God when he said, "We are not
big men. None of us is big, not even the missionaries. Only
Christ is big."

The proud have been humbled but not humiliated by shift-
ing the emphasis of their priorities. The ignorant have been
enriched, the miserable encouraged, and haters have been
changed to lovers of their fellow men.

Education has not made these changes; most Danis are still
illiterate. It is not civilization; they are yet only one step from
the Stone Age. Love has made the change. God is love, shed
abroad in the hearts of men yielded to Him.

18

The Putting Down of *Mongirat*

A LONE WOMAN trudged a hill path. Her dull face, framed by the knotted handles of a string bag, reflected that she walked without the companionship of lively thought.

Mendek put his hand on the arm of his companion and drew him into the cover of a clump of trees.

"Who is she?"

"She's Ogopak's wife from up in the valley. She makes strong *mongirat* [black magic] and has many cuts in her ears."

The woman passed and went down the other side of the hill. The men crept from hiding and chose another path. They preferred a circuitous road rather than the risk of bewitchment from a spell that the woman may have left in her wake.

Danis shunned a woman with cut ears. Each slit denoted a different involvement with sorcery, the hated *mongirat*, which was responsible for every death in the tribe.

Down at Tenggen Ambut, south of Ilu, the people were talking about *mongirat*. Black magic was strong down there at this time. Young Weren had died. His body had swelled from the magic inside him. All day the dead man's spirit had followed fellow tribesman, Maluk. Haunted by its oppressive presence, Maluk peered into the hut where the young man's mother caressed the body, while her tears splashed the lifeless face. She looked around at his approach.

Maluk reported to the village men, "I saw Weren's mother sitting beside his body. She looked this way and that. When she thought no one was looking, she stole a piece of his hair and buried it in the bush. See, here it is! She made *mongirat* and killed her son and took his hair to make more magic."

191

A murmur rumbled through the group of men and broke into cries of "Kill the witch! Kill her!"

Close relatives, screaming hate, arrowed the woman and threw her body where the river ran swiftest. The grief-stricken husband mourned his son and wife, who, named with the vilest, had been treated in death with the disrespect of a bitter enemy. He could give her no protection from a mob aroused for a witch hunt.

The missionaries suspected that Maluk had murdered the young man and named the mother as the death-promoting sorceress. But, who would hear the testimony of a woman with split ears against a man?

At every death bed, the dying man or woman was pressed to answer, "Who made the *mongirat?* Say her name."

If he were able, the dying would say, "So and so [naming a woman] saw me."

The blood of a pig was then squeezed on his head and shoulders to dispel the spirit sent by *mongirat*. But the woman who had been named was taken and tortured by stinging ants and sharp thorns. Sometimes her hair was burnt off to promote confession or to deter other women with a mind to making magic.

When a man died, his body, smeared with pig grease and decorated like a warrior with pig's tusks and feathers, was seated under a tree for all to see. A woman was clothed as though for her wedding. Mourning women beat their mud-plastered bodies and wailed, "The poor man is dead. He has no spirit left."

Sacrifices were made to benefit the departed spirit. Men discussed witchcraft and the responsible witch. Grass was cooked in the pits and strewn over the ground. If it turned brown, the woman named by the dying man was proved guilty of his death.

After the relatives had cremated their dead, men and girls crowded into the house of the deceased for a nightly *Deme deme* or courting dance, which culminated in sexual orgies.

During the daytime men went to hunt marsupials. With

CREMATION PYRE. The Danis cremate their dead.

many bagged, the woman's guilt was confirmed. If a few, the marsupials were scorched by flames in a divination rite to identify the true witch. The accused woman's ears were slit, and a copious flow verified her part in the death.

Sometimes the woman was arrowed, the most expedient method known for dealing with a traitor to the group. Such a death may appear to be cold-blooded, but the Danis had not heard of a harrowing wait in a comfortless cell for a wall and a firing squad in the grey dawn. Every culture has its own way of dealing with those regarded as traitors to its society.

At other times, any such humaneness was displaced by mob hysteria, resulting in clubbing, kicking, and beating a sorceress to a cruel death.

No man practiced *mongirat,* or *mum* as it was called in the Bokondini and Kelila areas. This was the women's craft. Certain men were mediums to prophesy or work as agents for the spirits. Such a man blew upon Warawi, a normal, intelligent man, to put an evil spirit within him.

With bow and arrow fixed for killing, Warawi came prancing, turning, and step dancing as he threatened the men racing after him.

"*Ap kumalik,* the man is mad! Grab him, somebody, grab him!" they shouted.

Outstripping the chasing men, he jumped over a precipice on the rocks below and ran on unhurt. The pursuers, not daring to jump to their death, scrambled down into the gorge. Near a village, others headed him off and bound him. In a short while he was again physically and mentally normal.

By the breath of an old man he had known superhumanity for a period. Those who have not been animists or lived in an animistic environment cannot understand, and few can accept these things. But those who have witnessed such manifestations recognize a tremendous power in evil. Animists have no difficulty in understanding the gospel account of the man of Gadara with the unclean spirit whom no man could bind with chains. They had frequently witnessed this demonic power. The manifestation that Paul had seen in Philippi they too had seen in the woman rushing through their meetings shouting, "Jesus, Jesus, Jesus!" They accept it for what the Scriptures say it is—the work of demons, while the contemporary Western philosopher looks for a mechanistic explanation.

The women's *mongirat,* while not producing demon possession, was believed to produce death through illness or violent accident. At the time of the Kelila fetish burning, the local Danis invited friends from the Dinggun group to a pig feast, where they intended to burn their "fighting magic." When they had all eaten, two hundred women, of their own volition, brought their magic and gave it to the missionaries. The Dani men went wild. Throwing their bodies about, they howled with excitement to be free from *mongirat.*

The missionaries opened the leaf-covered bundles to discover their secret.

"Don't touch it! Don't touch it!" the men pleaded.

"When Christ is in the heart, *mongirat* has no power over that one," the missionaries answered.

The bundles held no evil objects. No poison. No secret weapons for inserting foreign agents into a victim's body. Here a bit of hair, there some shiny quartz, a stone with a hole in it, some moss, and other bits of this and that.

As the flames consumed the women's *mongirat* and the men's fighting magic, the men cheered again, "*Mongirat* has gone. We shall die no more."

But the power of *mongirat* had not been destroyed with the burnings. Fear remained in the minds. In other areas all magic had not been burned and women had not lost their power to reproduce magic.

Tongirik, delirious with malaria, was taken from the hospital because, "There were too many women looking at me with their evil eyes."

Up the valley from the Bokondini at Wuniningga, a Christian boy, who had told the Bible stories in his village, died. As he died, he did not repeat a sorceress's name but said, "Do not cry for me. I am going to my Father God. We shall see each other again."

"But," the men reasoned, "if there is death, there must be *mongirat*."

They chose two women and pushed them into the river.

In a village twenty minutes walk from Mulia, a Dani died. As his body burned, some wanted to look for the witch.

"No," said Amalek, one of the Christian chiefs, "we won't talk about this anymore. We have finished with it."

Two days later Dave Scovill visited the village to investigate the reports that a sorceress had been killed by two irregular attendants at his Bible classes.

"Yes, Tuan, we shot her and hit her with an ax," they said.

"You see, it was like this," one of them continued. "This man that died had a gnawing pain in his stomach for months. He told us that his wife was eating him away with magic and that she would get Agarik too. When Agarik did get this pain, we chased this woman right down to the Jambi, six hours away."

"When we caught her, she admitted that she was killing these men," the other Bible school man added. "So we killed her. She is a bad woman. She would have killed many of our people."

"It is not right for God's people to kill even a sorceress." Scovill told them. "When we have faith in Christ, sorcery has no power against us."

"Did we do wrong to kill her, Tuan?" the first asked.

"We didn't know that this was not God's way," his friend joined in. "She was a true witch. As she died, we saw the evil spirit like grasshoppers come out of her mouth."

"What's this you say?" Scovill said sharply. "Don't lie to me. Tell me the truth. How can you possibly have seen grasshoppers come out of her mouth?"

"Tuan, we do not lie. Our eyes saw them," they protested. "Many times we see these things. You Tuans do not know from what we have been untied."

At Kelila Garnet Ericson met with a similar experience. At Mulia another missionary had seen men clubbing spirits which they said they could see escaping from a woman in a dying condition.

The skeptic rejects the inexplicable. But those who have witnessed the emancipation of a people from animism to Christianity can only rephrase the Dani's words:

"We Westerners do not know from what they have been untied." Because of his familiarity with these things, the animist does not query the possibility of spirits entering the swine that plunged down the hill into the sea at Gennesaret.

Although the actual objects used in producing black magic —stones, bits of hair—in themselves held no potency to harm, both the women's *mongirat* and the men's fighting magic were weapons directed at the mind. They produced a will-dominating fear. The spirit medium has absolute confidence in the power of his magic. His practices are not a string of deceptions. There are too often power and results in his sorcery.

Black magic is Satan's counteraction to God's perfect will for man, made in the image of God, and designed to know the mind of Christ. In his attempt to spoil the works of God, Satan operates on the mind of man, perverting his concept of God, distorting his imagination and misrepresenting his purpose in life, until he is completely out of alignment with God's eternal purpose for him. Having full control of the mind, Satan can twist a man to his bidding.

The animist looks for a reason in all that affects his life. He attributes the cause to spirits, either working against him if the consequence is bad, or for him if the effect is good. Any good that befalls him is because he has lived within the boundaries of appeasement rites and sacrifices, doing nothing to evoke the spirits to anger.

An animist, who does not look for the how of a certain accident or happening but only for the why can see nothing but the work of spirits. Where the activities of demons begin and end in the lives of men who have given themselves to spirit worship is not for the nonanimist to say. However, the Bible student has the authority to declare that the ultimate blinding of the mind is the deceiving work of Satan.

Charles Horne was able to explain this to some Dani men when they came to him saying "Tuan, we cannot hold our services in the open air where the women have their market. They may have left *mongirat* in the grass and in the stones. If we sit there it will enter our bodies."

"*Mongirat* is in your minds and nowhere else," Horne told them. "Whatever means the women use to operate their magic, the result is the hold it has over your minds. The burning of the media of *mongirat* has not killed it. It still lives in your hearts in the form of fear. Break that and you have broken the power of *mongirat*. How can you break this? By obeying Christ and obeying God's Word. It says, 'Let the mind of Christ be in you,' then fear will go out, 'for God has not given us a spirit of fear.' Knowing Christ and making Him sovereign in our lives will overcome fear because we have confidence that God is greater than the power of evil."

But it was not until after a conference of missionaries was held that Dani men and women, observing how the European men and women had fellowship together, began to intermingle without fear and superstition in practical demonstration of their confidence in God.

At a Dani church service following the conference, Unak, one of the leaders, said to the concourse, "You men, you come to church and you don't know where your wives are sitting. You women, you don't know where your men are. I shall show you the way in which we should sit." Taking his wife by the arm he lead her to a place, saw her seated, and sat beside her.

"Now," he continued, "This is the way we shall sit in church."

And they did. Next Sunday and those following, the men sat with their women. Man and wife sat together around the Lord's table. In fellowship with God the fear of *mongirat* disappeared.

Of their own volition the Danis introduced a new pattern into village life. In the Bible school village at Bokondini the *matno,* or men's house, ceased to be merely the men's sleeping quarters and a council chamber for spirit worship and war discussion. It was divided into a living apartment for the leader and his family, and a large common room where men could congregate to talk about church progress and personal problems. It was also open to the women when all gathered for Bible study and prayer. The former women's houses around the *matno* now became family homes where the husband lived as head and led in his family's worship.

Others began to copy this pattern.

It was in bringing women into united fellowship in Christ that fear in the power of sorcery was dispelled. Only after the putting down of *mongirat* could the Dani woman take her rightful place as cherished wife and mother in the home. Again as the Danis put Christ in the center of their focus, the problem was dealt with, and family life moved back to what God had intended it to be.

19

The Danis Reach Beyond

In October, 1963, Dave Scovill and Stan Sadlier with ten Dani volunteers flew to a strategic airstrip and walked three days into the valley to the west which the people called Naltja. Trekking up through rain forests and winding around the side of a mountain, they entered the Naltja garden area. Men and women, working among their potatoes, raised their heads as the carrier line went through and then turned back to their work.

The missionary party pitched camp, erected temporary huts, and started work on the airstrip, but still the Naltjas ignored them. They brought no food to sell and made no offer to work.

The Naltja men fought hard and their women worked hard, but their gardens were few and poor. What had appeared to be large villages from the air were mainly empty houses vacated on account of death or other unexplained reasons. The people wore dog teeth necklaces and pierced and decorated their noses in the same manner as the Kiwilok people and those spreading down on the southern slopes of the Star Mountains into Papua. The missionaries had hoped to find a corresponding dialectical similarity, but unfortunately the language was unrelated.

The Danis had gone into the Naltja valley with the keen desire to preach Christ. What they could not say with their tongues they said with their lives. Somehow they made the Naltjas understand that they too had once feared evil spirits, but now through faith in God were freed from their power.

The days grew from weeks into months, and still most Naltjas chose to ignore the newcomers. Fears of the unknown and false conjecture about that of which they were ignorant held them back from friendship. To them the dolls in the Lockhart girls' arms were the shrunken bodies of their parents' unwanted children.

Malnutrition restricted the output of the few who worked. After twenty minutes of half-hearted effort they came to the missionary with outstretched hands asking for the day's pay.

"Let's forget about them and do the work ourselves," the Danis offered.

The twenty-two Danis taken into Naltja by Dave Cole to relieve the original party did the work of a hundred men. They scraped four or five feet of mud from the surface of the airstrip, laid a foundation with huge rocks, and covered it with barrow load after barrow load of gravel.

"With our limited equipment I didn't expect to build that strip with less than four to five hundred men," Cole said.

They worked from daylight until dark, and sometimes when the moon was brilliant, well into the night. In all, the Dani lay-Christians made an invaluable contribution to the opening of the Naltja work. And now both Dani pastors and missionaries who have worked together through seven years of alternating despair and encouragement are at last beginning to see some signs of the birth of a church.

In a further outreach, other Dani men from Kelila and Bokondini accompanied a Dutch missionary to an area beyond Wolo and outside the Dani group to help him establish a Christian witness for a Dutch missionary society. The Danis were learning that race and denomination are not barriers when men need Christ.

When the fetish-burning movement first began, word of it reached the Nggems down at Lake Archbold. Responsible men walked up to Kelila to hear the straight talk about this new thing. Some brought their fetishes and burned them in the missionary's backyard. Nggem family groups moved in to hear the teaching and lived near the Kelila church for weeks at a time. With them they brought malaria and scabies from the

NALTJA HOUSE. A Naltja house as seen by the missionaries
when they first advanced into the territory

low country. With an antimalaria campaign the government
tried to prevent the spread of the disease, but it was already
introduced, and the Nggems would not be stayed. The missionaries treated case after case until their medicines were exhausted. Influenza followed and struck many in a weakened
condition. Forty of the Christians at Bokondini died. Pastors
too lost children, wives, and parents, but the church did not
lose its faith. The proven truth of Scripture was a bulwark
against despair. There was no thought that God had failed.
He had never promised them freedom from trouble, but sus-
tenance in the midst of trial, and they found Him sufficient.

Unak, the supervising pastor at Bokondini, whose chubby
infant son had died in the epidemic, bowed to the sovereignty
of God and went down again to the Nggem valley to help
Pastor Yowan, who had been given the responsibility of evangelizing the Nggems. These people built their church on the

ridge which the missionaries had climbed when they had begun work at Archbold. From here they had first looked down
on Bokondini. Now Bokondini men were going back down
the same trail which had brought the missionaries into their
country, not with spears and arrows but with the teaching of
eternal life!

That which the missionaries envisaged when they shifted
camp from Lake Archbold to establish headquarters at Bokondini was becoming a reality. The lake people were now the
outreach of the indigenous church. This missionary drive has
not been confined to the preaching of pastors or enthusiastic
individuals, but instead a community effort has prepared a
highway for the gospel advance. A hundred Kelila Christians
went out east toward Wolo and built an airstrip at Winum.
Now pastors and missionaries visit this place frequently, and
these Danis too receive regular Bible teaching.

In its missionary endeavor the church has not forgotten
Wolo. Since the station was evacuated in 1963, the church has
not ceased to pray for a way back. Pilots flying across Wolo
brought back reports that mission homes had been burnt, gardens and fruit trees destroyed.

Tamene and Emelugun had walked in occasionally to test
the climate of local feeling for the evacuees' return. A minority
welcomed them, but large hostile groups rejected any suggestion of a renewal of Christian activity within their boundaries. Mbiri, who had seen Tamene's wife's miraculous escape
from drowning, and who had acknowledged, "Now we know
that you love us," to the missionaries, had nevertheless turned
away from their message. Acting against the convictions of
his heart he had driven out the Christians and had stood
against their reentry.

Early in 1964 he could resist the Spirit of God no longer
and walked across the limestone mountains into Kelila. He
spoke with the missionaries and Wolo Christian leaders. "Will
you come back and teach us the true way?" he asked.

Mbiri represented only one section of the valley, and although chiefs of other areas strongly opposed his overtures to

the Christians, leaders returned with him to work among his group.

Pastors and trainees, comprised of both Wolos and local western Danis, were sent by the Bokondini and Kelila divisional church council into Wolo for two and three months at a time. With their families they lived close to the people, instructing them in the Scripture and illustrating its practical application by their daily living. Although surrounded by sporadic fighting between the Baliem, Ilugwa, and Wolo; harassed by threats and warnings; and wearied by constant friction, the church grew in numbers and spiritual strength.

Over in the east, the Wolo people still followed hard after their old ways. Hostilities were fanned by two brothers who lived on the Ilugwa-Wolo trail. When two Ilugwa men visited Bokondini and Kelila with the pastors, they were caught in an influenza epidemic. On their return, the disease developed and they died. This gave the two warmongers their opportunity.

"The Bokondini-Kelila people have made black magic against these men," they claimed.

They massed their troops and came against the pastors. The Christians and adherents met them and drove them off.

One of the brothers, Titlok, with other big chiefs, had established himself in a stronghold on the high ranges towards the Baliem. There had been times when he had been nearly persuaded to throw in his lot with the Christians. He had accepted missionaries' medication and on their behalf resisted the attack on the station at the beginning of the Wolo program. Gradually he has hardened his heart and spurned the truth. Now in the bravado of his rejection, trying to outwit his nagging conscience, boost his ego, and rally followers, he boasts, "My father has killed Jesus—who are you following now?" Blinded by deceit he has moved further and further from the place of repentance. He has sold his birthright—salvation in Christ—for passing power. Will he too, like Esau, look for a place of repentance and not find it?

Despite threats, the pastors made spasmodic thrusts up into

the Ilugwa valley where the fighting which drove the Christians out of Wolo commenced. At first there had been no unanimity among the villages in the requests that had come through for pastors to visit them. Some, openly hostile, declared their preference for their old ways. In answer the pastor took a young banana shoot and cut off the root. Planting the top and root beside each other, he told them, "Watch these! One has life and power in it, and the other hasn't." As the villagers watched the one plant wither and die and the other grow and develop, they read the message which the pastor had written them in this parable.   Towards the end of 1964 a group of "big" men from this section of the Ilugwa came to the church leaders saying that they were convinced that the Christian way was right and wanted pastors to come teach them.

"We have a place where the plane can come down. If you will come, we will work on it and make a strip," they said.

In May 1965, after tremendous effort to split and clear away heavy boulders, the strip was smooth and hard. The Danis received well-deserved praise from the Indonesian air official who flew with the MAF operational manager, on the first landing.

With Dani-initiated strip building widening the churches' outreach, the pastors kept the missionary torch burning. Some went considerable distances from their homes even at risk to their lives, preaching and teaching.

Gradually Titlock and his compatriots began to realize that the Christians with no personal involvements in the fighting wished to be freed from participation. Pelelek, the man who had arrowed Wal Turner, was one. He stood against the leaders saying, "There is something in this teaching. I want to hear and learn it." Finally recognizing that the Christians were nonaggressive, Titlok let them go unmolested to and from the meeting places.

Chief Mbiri and other paternal group leaders committed their lives to Christ. Despite the pressure of opposition, they won through and established a witness. They had found that eternal life was not immortality, or something waiting for them after death, but life operating in them now.

On September 14, 1965, large groups of Wolos from Bokondini and Kelila walked back into Wolo by the trail over which, three years earlier, many had fled from persecution looking for a new life in a new land. Some were Wolos returning to their own country for the first time since the evacuation. Bruised and blood-smeared Wolo is slowly turning to God.

Although the outreach of the Dani church has been an indigenous effort, thrilling those who have seen it expand, every spearhead has been met with opposition and frustration: hostility at Wolo, indifference at Naltja, rugged terrain, and epidemics in the Nggem country. But Dani drive, harnessed by the Holy Spirit, is breaking down all barriers. The energy which they once expended in fighting and animistic ritualism they now spend to develop the church.

The Danis, like most emerging groups, have seen that if they themselves are to be able teachers within the framework of an indigenous church, they must become educated.

Of course, at this stage, a formal education cannot be given to all. To achieve the best end results, primary schools were opened taking six and seven-year-olds. However, sixteen-year-old Lematin was determined to gain what he could. He had learned to read and write in the first literacy classes, and when a regular school for first graders opened at the center near his village, he hung through the windows of the school room in an effort to learn all he could from their lessons. Impressed by his eagerness, the teacher could not refuse him enrollment with the children.

Atlenggen was another young man who was not contented with the crumbs of knowledge offered him, and when given the opportunity, did not scorn to take his place in school with younger children. His aim was to enter Bible school so that he could teach his own people. At night he learned English from the missionaries. Learning from the government personnel at Bokondini, he became a fluent speaker in Indonesian, the country's national language. Thus, he took a vital part in the

Sunday services held for coastal people employed on the government station at Bokondini. One of these employees was a Sengge man who had walked with Veldhuis, Dawson, and Bond from the Baliem to Lake Archbold. There is no finality to a man's experience; he enlarges his experience, takes what he has received to another in need. The Dani man, having learned from God, teaches a group including the Sengge man who first brought him spiritual teaching.

At this time young people have opportunities for education which had not been previously spoken of in the highland valleys. In 1961 the mission societies working in West Irian formed the Missions Fellowship. Members of The Missions Fellowship (TMF) in West Irian include the Australian Baptist Missionary Society, Christian & Missionary Alliance, Missionary Aviation Fellowship, Regions Beyond Missionary Union, The Evangelical Alliance Mission, and the Unevangelized Fields Mission. Through this they have been able to make a common approach to the government in such matters as education by forming a Missions Education Foundation, which is headed by an Indonesian Christian. As the government requires all teachers to be Indonesian, this foundation assists in recruiting teachers as well as administering the education program in TMF areas.

Since that time, primary schools have taken children through the normal grades. Then in 1968 a teacher training secondary school opened at Bokondini, which was chosen by The Missions Fellowship for its centrality. Among the first thirty students were some from Wissel Lakes and the north coast as well as from the highland areas. By the following year the intake had doubled and of the sixty-four students enrolled at the beginning of 1969, two were girls—one an Indonesian and the other a Dani.

The buildings, which have been designed to eventually accommodate 120 students and a staff of four, have been erected by national carpenters trained in mission schools.

Mrs. Malonda, the first headmistress, is a graduate from the University of Makassar. The three other teachers on the staff, like the principal, come from the island of Sulawesi. A major responsibility for the local missionary staff in the curriculum of this training school is instruction in Christian education.

After completing a minimum of nine years' schooling, the students will return to their home areas as primary school teachers. Probably some will go to the coast and enter the Bible institute planned for the Evangelical Church of West Irian. Bert Power is in charge of this program. Leadership courses are in view, and various training projects which will also help meet the institute's running costs. All courses will be conducted in Indonesian. Most young people who have completed their schooling in Indonesian do not readily adapt to attending a vernacular Bible School. And if Dani and other Christians are to exercise leadership and influence in their country, it is essential that they receive their training in Indonesian.

Another project planned by the intermissions fellowship is the opening of a technical school at Ilu in 1972. Although most of the staff will be Indonesian, an official request has been made for a foreign qualified technical teacher to serve as a missionary.

A tremendous task lies ahead of the Dani church. The thousands who have cut themselves away from their old religion need nurturing in the new teaching which they have chosen. The weak need encouraging, the illiterate need teaching, the gifted need training, and there are those who still need evangelizing. The great Shangri-la Valley of the central Danis, as a community, still resists the gospel, although within the tribe individuals and family groups are following Christ. The evangelizing of the Central Baliem Valley may well be the unaided responsibility of the west Dani church.

Their lost eternal life has been restored to them. With it has come life, outpouring and overflowing. The exuberant mass movement has given place to a steady learning and preaching of truth. In these Stone Age valleys, the gospel of Christ has turned villainy into righteousness, hate to love, cruelty to kindness, and bondage to freedom. Proud men have subjected themselves to God and have become humble and able to be used by Him.

"When you missionaries first came," said a trainee pastor, "I wanted only your tomato and corn seed so that I could sell produce and get many cowrie shells. I wanted axes and cloth and the other things which you had. Now these things don't matter: I want only the things of Christ."

It is upon such men, who hold this single-minded philosophy, that the future of the Dani church depends. The political pressures on a country pushed prematurely forward to take its place in a competitive world leave an indent upon its national church.

While the traditional missionary outreach within the world appears to be shrinking and the pioneering conditions are fast disappearing, there are still vital responsibilities for the expatriate missionary within the framework of the established national church. Although the Danis have been building an indigenous church capable of self-government, and although these Stone Age men made whole in Christ are deciding domestic issues for themselves, they still look to the American and Australian church to send men who will help them with translation, literature, secular and spiritual education, and medical aid. These men will not be able to dominate nor dictate to the Dani leaders. They will work side by side with them. It will not be the Dani church gathered around American and Australian leadership, but Danis, Americans and Australians serving Christ in a common fellowship.

And so in self-propagation, the great western Dani church, having caught the missionary vision, goes forward. Pastor Unak spoke for them all when he said. "We are not following a man, we are following God."